Beverly Almond -
An Ageless Adventurer

Beverly Almond - An Ageless Adventurer

Beverly Anne Hamlin

Cover design by Rob Lancaster

ISBN: 1517721318
ISBN 13: 9781517721312

Foreword

It is not an unusual thing for someone to appreciate or love their mother, or even to be proud of her. It is perhaps less usual to have a mother with a life story that is so compelling and inspiring that it simply must be told, and one that people in a wide variety of places, ages and backgrounds strongly urge be told.

That is the case for my mother, and since I am one who has known her longer than most, I decided that I would try to do the job.

Of course the major challenge with knowing her so well is that objectivity is impossible. Nevertheless, I have tried as much as possible to let her tell her own story, using taped interviews and her own letters, as well as scrapbooks and albums. Happily for me as I tackled this project, I have had a wealth of material to draw on as both my grandmother and my mother were keepers of papers. Thus there is much primary source material to draw on – ranging from baby books and school essays to annual Christmas letters, and a great deal of correspondence. In any case, the basic facts speak for themselves.

In my view, perhaps the most interesting thing about Beverly Anne Kitchen Almond is that she was born into a life of comfort and privilege, but chose for herself a life of challenge, giving, and adventure. At several key moments in her life she had options for ease or a simpler way – but she rejected that path for a more rigorous one because she wanted to make a difference, have a part, and give her best. Also, one of her strongest qualities is curiosity – and that has always led her to interesting places and people, and to questioning things.

Because of this, she has had a life rich in experiences and people beyond anything she could have imagined, and is still beloved and found interesting by a vast array of friends of many kinds in several countries.

Contents

Acknowledgements

Having now written my first book, I understand why authors feel the need to express thanks to so many people for the help given to them as they pursued their project. I find myself in exactly that position as I reflect back on what has happened to make this story come to life.

Not only do I have the gift of all the papers saved by my grandmother and mother to draw on, but also the genealogical records produced by my aunt Hope Ayer from her research. Thanks are due also to Wendy Prindle Berlind, Betsy Wilson and other relatives for contributing helpful perspective, clarification, and information at various times.

Elizabeth Lancaster, my sister Betsy, was a careful and helpful reader and added much with her insights, memories, corrections, and also help on some computer questions.

My brother-in-law Rob Lancaster took a huge load off my mind when he agreed to work on the cover of the book, and I am delighted with what he created. He also helped greatly with proofreading and fact checking.

Jennifer Lancaster, my "favorite niece", contributed her recollections of staying with my mother for some months, and also worked on the back cover text.

My very well-read and honest friend Sarah Cummer was very helpful in reading an early draft of the book and giving perspective from outside the family.

Bryan, my husband, has been a pillar of strength – providing lots of patient encouragement, carefully reading and re-reading many times and giving excellent suggestions, and believing in the project enthusiastically from the start. He also carefully scanned masses of old family photos.

And of course my mother has been her usual extraordinary self. She put up with hours of interviews and questions, even when the topics were delicate or even painful to recall. She generously opened her life and heart to my probing, and answered and shared honestly. She has carefully read several drafts, and always had feedback to give, typos to correct, and appreciation to express.

To all these and other dear family and friends, and to all those who encouraged me and kept asking when The Book would be done – THANK YOU. Here it is! I absolutely couldn't have done it without you all.

Any errors that remain in this book are mine, and are in spite of all the excellent help I've been given.

Introduction

I f you drive up Baldwin Hill in the lovely Berkshire Hills of western Massachusetts, turn into the driveway of a modest ranch-style home and go inside to be greeted by the lady of the house, a petite woman in her late 90s, you will always be given a warm and sincere welcome. It is a simple home, comfortable though modestly decorated, and your hostess is likely wearing her typical simple outfit of a skirt and blouse. It doesn't take long to understand that she is doing very well for someone of her age; and the fact that she lives alone, still drives locally, enjoys baking cookies, bread, pies, and cakes for others, and is active in her church and local politics, all attest to the fact that she is rather special.

If you look around carefully, however, you will see many clues that there is more to this lady than healthy active old age. There are piles of books, and crossword puzzles in the process of being solved. You will see a variety of artwork and artifacts on display – such items as an Arab coffee pot, an old map of Buckinghamshire in England, a painting from Denmark. There is a Muslim prayer rug hanging on the wall, a basket of correspondence from around the world waiting to be answered; and it doesn't take long to spot the medal and citation from former British Prime Minister Gordon Brown sitting on a table near the door. Clearly there is more to this woman, Beverly Almond, than one might first imagine. There is indeed a fascinating story to be told!

CHAPTER 1

Childhood

Beverly Anne Kitchen was born at 7:30 am on July 8th, 1918, in Great Neck, Long Island, New York; the first child of her proud parents – Victor and Elsie Rodman Kitchen. She was delivered at home, 65 Arleigh Rd., by Dr. E.E. Stewart. She weighed 7lb. 4oz. and was 21 inches long, with blue eyes and 'golden' hair, as recorded in her baby book.

Wonderfully, both this baby book and a journal in which her mother wrote the details of her arrival still exist, so quoting from that journal provides the best description of the event, and the mixture of joy, challenges and sorrow that wove through the first weeks of this child's life. It also highlights the delicate state new mothers of privilege were considered to be in for some time after giving birth in those days.

In Elsie's words, "At 10 pm July 7th Sunday night, my sister Bessie was here and Vic was guarding the armory (his military duty), when very slight pains began. At 3:15 am I called the Dr., at 3:30, Miss Whittle, the nurse, and at 4:00, Vic. Miss Whittle arrived at about 4:45, and real pain started at 6 o'clock. Dr. Stuart arrived at 6:45, Vic at seven, and the baby at 7:30. Bessie stayed until Tuesday morning, and then Mamma came Tuesday afternoon and stayed until Saturday morning. On Sunday I sat up in bed (6 days after birth), and Mary (Vic's sister) and her family came for lunch. I saw them and later Helen Clarke (her best friend). Mamma came back Monday, and on Tuesday 16th morning we had news of Papa's death, and Mamma went right home (to New Jersey), but was very brave. Wednesday I sat up in a chair for half an hour. Friday was Papa's funeral at 4:30 in the afternoon.

"Beverly had her first tub bath on Thursday, July 19th. I bathed her on Saturday, July 26th, Miss Whittle left Monday, July 29th. [This seems to indicate that the nurse had bathed her for almost the first three weeks.] I sat up an hour on the 14th day, two hours the 15th day, etc., and came downstairs Sunday, July 27th. The first week after Miss Whittle left the baby was pretty good, but the next week she was upset by the heat – the worst on record, 101F in the shade in New York (NY)." In fact the record of 104F in Long Island City, NY at that time stands to this day.

A letter, written by Elsie to Beverly in 1968 for her fiftieth birthday, reflects back on that time of her birth and all the stresses she experienced. "The nurse I had for 3 weeks was not the one Dr. Stewart had planned, and Rosline, the maid, couldn't abide her, so there was friction from the first, for you, in the household. It all made me jittery, which I am convinced gave you the ceaseless colic you had for 6 months, looking very healthy all the while, but crying day and night."

Continuing from Elsie's notebook, "No wonder Beverly had colic, and I didn't have enough milk for her. Papa's death, then Rosline kept threatening to leave; I was worried about Mamma's financial affairs after Papa died; my sister Carol went to a sanatorium (at Saranac Lake, NY for tuberculosis), a friend had an operation, and Rosline went to hospital with flu which developed into pneumonia. Also, my laundress was here half sick on Saturday and didn't appear again for ten days."

Elsie refers to Rosline going to hospital with influenza in October. Then in November Elsie's brother Bay, little Beverly's godfather, was sick with the flu at the time of her christening and wasn't present for the service. This flu was in fact the Spanish influenza epidemic that ravaged around the world in 1918-1920, killing at least 50 million people (about 4% of the world's population), the biggest natural disaster ever for humanity. Following as it did from the massive loss of life in WWI, it was truly a global tragedy. It was very fortunate that neither baby Beverly nor her parents contracted it.

Beverly and her mother

Despite this tumultuous start, Little Beverly was indeed a very fortunate little girl, born into a large, loving, extended family, and in a very comfortable neighborhood – the Kensington section of Great Neck, a newly developing and well-to-do town on the Long Island Railroad, and an easy ride from New York City (NYC). This community was where F. Scott Fitzgerald lived and where *The Great Gatsby* was set, all at about the time Beverly was growing up there. Her early years were indeed the Roaring Twenties!

Not only that, but both of her parents' families – the Kitchens (her father's) and the Rodmans (her mother's) were true 'WASPS' (White Anglo-Saxon Protestants). Ancestors on the Rodman side were descended from two Mayflower Pilgrims, and several ancestors from both sides fought in the American Revolution, making the ladies of the family eligible for membership in the DAR (Daughters of the American Revolution). It was certainly a background of both privilege and deep roots in American history.

Her father, Victor Constant Kitchen, worked in advertising in NYC as a partner in Doyle, Kitchen and McCormick, and he commuted daily on the railroad to his office located at 42nd St. and Fifth Ave. Vic (as he was called) had one sister, Mary Lippincott, who was older and who lived next door in Great Neck with her husband, Wells, and their three sons. These neighboring houses had been built for the siblings as wedding presents from their parents.

The family was comfortably well-off, and had several people who worked for them. One was the afore-mentioned big-hearted Jamaican housekeeper Rosline Henry, present from before Beverly's birth and for several years after. She was much beloved by the family and helped with the children as well as household duties and cooking. Other people did laundry, gardening, served at dinner parties, and so on; and later they had a governess, or nanny.

Beverly's mother, Elsie Fairfield Rodman Kitchen, was one of a family of seven, six girls and then one boy – named Beverly, after whom baby Beverly was named. He was usually called Bay, but he had another nickname, Bevo, which came from the name of a 'near-beer'. This was a malt beverage with no alcohol popular in America from 1916 on, especially during Prohibition. Little Beverly not only got her first name from him but was also often called Bevo by family and friends. She is also called Bev by many, and will be referred to as Beverly or Bev in this book.

Beverly didn't know her Grandfather Rodman, who had died eight days after she was born, or her Grandmother Rodman, who died about eight months later. She did know her Kitchen grandparents, and all of her many aunts and her Uncle Bay well, as they all lived not too far away in the New York area. Family photos from the first years of her life show her with both Kitchen grandparents, Aunt Mary Lippincott and her sons, on the Kitchen side. On the Rodman side there are photos of the Janeways – her Aunt Carol, aka "Auntie Cuckoo", and Uncle Will, and their children. He was a doctor and they lived on Staten Island.

There is a delightful letter written to little Beverly on the day of her birth by her grandfather, Dr. Joseph M. W. Kitchen, welcoming her to the world. He starts by addressing her as "Granddaughter dearest" and then explains how he has been interested in her "for some time past, not knowing that you were he, she, or it . . . I am almost tickled to death that you was 'laid' a girl, kid, which fact will be a joyous matter of cackling to a wide circle – and a matter of alleviation to your rather cocky young cousin, Richard Lippincott, when he finds that a certain 'disjointment' of his nasal protuberance has occurred. You have a right smart chance of being considerably loved by many folks, including your most aged grandparent who includes these presents." He then advises her on her diet, saying, "Believe me that mother's milk is a far better nutrient than lactic production of bovine extraction." It is signed "fondly and adoringly, your grandfather". This was more than just kind grandfatherly advice as he was an expert on the purity of milk. See more about him in the next chapter.

Beverly at age 2, 1920

Bev's sister Myra was born on October 26th, 1921, and sometime after Myra's birth the Kitchens hired a nurse/governess, Frances Stapleton from Canada, to look after the girls. Beverly recalls this woman with a shudder, as she felt very strongly that the nanny adored Myra, but did not like her and treated her badly. "I was unhappy in her reign. She was tall and straight and had iron gray short hair, and she was strict! She favored Myra much more than me and that was tough. She may have spanked me, but I don't remember for sure."

Certainly life was never boring around this little girl. There are many stories recounted, some by her and some by her mother, of her mischievous exploits as a child. The most oft-told is of the time when the neighbor across the street called to say that little Beverly (about two years old and supposedly napping at the time) was walking up and down the flower box outside the 2nd floor window above the front door, stark naked! Rosline was sent to get her safely back in without making her fall, Beverly remembers. Perhaps her mother was either too upset or afraid of startling her if she had gone up.

Bev tells of pranks she did with another friend, Dotty (Doris) Knighton. Once they went to the home of a neighbor with chickens and let them all out of the cage, and they got into big trouble. Another time when there were some workmen doing some kind of job at their house, Beverly and Dotty found the men's lunch boxes in the garage and ate all their sandwiches.

It is clear from other stories that this young lady had strong opinions and a strong will. She tells, with great feeling still in her late 90s, of how much she hated both bones in fish and strings in beans, and how she managed to hide them in her hand or napkin during meals, and then stash them by the radiator in the dining room by shoving them through the cracks in the metal radiator cover. She got away with this until the heat was turned on and the stench got strong! She also recalls depositing spoonfuls of oatmeal into the toilet to dispose of them.

Beverly recounted other childhood adventures. "I know another thing I did when I was in the 'terrible twos'. Somebody had left a bottle of aspirin on top of a high chest of drawers. I pulled the drawers out partway and climbed up and ate half the bottle of aspirin! They had to have the doctor come and pump my stomach out. I think I did make life interesting for mother.

"One time I didn't want to go to school and I'd heard that if you took a whisk broom and rubbed it on your chest it would look like measles, so I did that and it worked for a day."

Next-door neighbor, Adelaide Garney, was a good friend. In an interview done in 2007, Beverly told about that relationship. "Adelaide was just between Myra and me in age. So one week she and I would be teamed up and Myra would be the great enemy, and the next week Adelaide and Myra would be great friends and I'd be the enemy. There was a metal link fence and a hedge between their yard and ours. We had a tree in our yard and the branches went over to their side. So we built a tree-house in that tree, and we could go up or down steps on each side to get to each other's houses – without having to go ALL the way to the front and around the hedge! So we spent some happy times up there."

Bev added, "We also used to do things in the neighborhood, playing games like kick-the-can, hide and seek, 'king of the mountain', and all that stuff. And I remember in the Fall, when the leaves were being burned, we'd put potatoes in the ashes to bake them."

Another story which, although it happened later on when Beverly was about 13 years old, also involved Adelaide and took place while they were visiting the Garneys' place in Montauk, Long Island. There was a group of kids hanging out, and they got the idea of playing a prank on a local business that did plumbing and heating work and had those words painted on the roof. One night this mischievous crew sent Beverly up a ladder to add the letter 'C' to the sign – thus making it read "Plumbing and Cheating"!

When Beverly was five (1923) she started Kindergarten at the Great Neck Preparatory School, a small private school at the other end of Great Neck. She remembers that her teacher was Miss Cook, and she was amused that she as a Kitchen had a teacher called Cook. Elsie Kitchen said to Miss Cook once that her daughter was bossy, and Miss Cook replied that "Oh no, Mrs. Kitchen, we say she's a little leader!" She remembers uniforms for that school were a navy blue serge skirt that scratched, and a heavy blouse with a big sailor collar and long sleeves. She thinks there may also have been long dark stockings. A letter from the Headmaster to her parents after her first grade year reads as follows, "She has worked well and has developed into a beautiful reader . . . She is an inspiration to the others of her class, but has to be curbed in her enthusiasm of dictating to others."

Extraordinarily, a folder full of writing Beverly did in 3rd grade (October, 1926), has survived, and one piece is about ancient Mesopotamia. Showing unwitting prescience, Beverly wrote: "The Tigris and Euphrates Rivers flow into the Persian Gulf. Bagdad [sic] is on the Tigris River. Basra is on the Shat-el-Arab. People living in the region of these two rivers eat mutton, dates and bread. These people make the famous Persian rugs. Much traveling is done by caravans. The houses are made of brick or clay and have flat roofs. One may see many palm trees. The people wear loose robes. The land is dry and barren." Mostly accurate and quite impressive knowledge for her age. It seems they studied ancient civilizations that year as there are also essays on ancient Greece and Egypt. Who could have predicted then how the Middle East would come to be such an important part of Beverly's life?

Four years after Myra's arrival, a third sister, Hope, was born in 1925, when Beverly was seven years old. She recalls that clearly. "I can remember very well sitting at the end of the kitchen table in Great Neck, and Myra was next to me and somebody came along and said 'Dr. Stewart has just come along with a little black bag and brought you a baby sister.' That's what I remember about the advent of Hope, whom we usually called Hopie. I think my reaction was curiosity. It's amazing how clearly I remember that moment – exactly where we were sitting and how someone came and told us that. I think we were eating supper."

A charming trio – Beverly, baby Hope and Myra in 1925

Beverly attended Great Neck Preparatory School through 4th grade, and then began 5th grade in the nearby public school to which she walked. "The headmistress, Miss Johnson, was very nice. I remember liking my 5th grade teacher very much. She and Miss Johnson had a house together, and they used to come to our house for meals sometimes. I went there through 8th grade."

In 9th grade she moved on to Great Neck High School which she attended for two years. Mention of this school brought forth the well-remembered words of the school song from which Bev then sang several lines: " 'Through the four long years of high school, we strive along our way, and as we pass throughout them, we sing a doleful lay, la la la . . . when once we were defenders of the orange and the blue.' I think I was an orange," Bev added.

A close friend from her days at the Great Neck public schools was Martha Jane Yale, who is remembered most fondly. The Yale family had a summer place in the Thousand Islands in upstate New York. Bev went there with them for a visit for at least two summers and seems to have had a wonderful time, judging by her letters home.

Another good friend she had in Great Neck was Ethel Durant, daughter of Will and Ariel, the famous chroniclers of American history with their multi-volume *Story of Civilization*. Beverly only realized many years later that Ethel was Jewish, because she remembers having a sense as a child that Jews and Catholics were not people her family would normally have been friends with.

Not much is remembered by Beverly about larger events in the country such as the Depression, or its impact on her life. She does remember her father making a joke about how just when they'd bought a new stove, the stock market failed, so how would they pay for it? But she clearly remembers it being said in a joking way.

Other memories from the Great Neck era: "Kensington was an enclave, and down at the bottom of the hill there was a club with tennis courts and a swimming pool, and we used to go there in summer when we weren't in New Hampshire. There were quite a few kids in the neighborhood. There was a girl whose house was behind ours called Gladys Parker (always called Golly), and she was a friend of Hopie's – a bit younger generation."

A birthday party on the lawn, 1920

She recalled with a groan, "Oh, painful – Mother used to take us into New York City on Saturdays. There were Ernest Schelling Concerts for Children, I think in Carnegie Hall. I hated that because I wanted to be climbing trees or something like that. I was definitely a tomboy – no question about that! I must have had dolls, I'm sure I did, but I don't remember them. Then, when I was a bit older, I remember going to see Katherine Hepburn in a play." Beverly was a huge fan of Ms. Hepburn then, and still is.

"We had a maid named Kay who was an absolutely wonderful person. We kept in touch with her after she got married, and up until she died. She was Polish and later married a man called Ralph Gill. We were great friends. She used to have these magazines with all sorts of stories about movie stars, true love, and all kinds of junk, and I used to go in her room and read those. She came from a large family with quite a few kids and I used to feel sorry for her. I felt they needed things.

"So another thing I did – Mother and Daddy were having a dinner party, and the ladies all put their coats and purses on Mother's bed. I went through them and took some money out of one of the purses and gave it to Kay the next day. She immediately went and told Mother, and it turned out it was the purse of Mother's best friend, Aunt Helen Clark, who lived just further along Arleigh Road from us. I had to go and apologize to her, and that was awful because I was very fond of them. I'm not sure I knew whose purse it was I'd taken the money from. It was just the first $5 or $10 bill I came across.

"As for my sister Myra, sometimes we were good friends and sometimes we fought. We were in separate rooms normally, but one time we had to share as there were guests. We were really fighting and I pushed her so hard she fell and hit her head. I was really scared then. Another time one of us went out the window of that room and held onto the window sill and then dropped down onto the ground. I don't remember which one of us it was who did that, but we were OK. Sometimes we had actual physical fights, other times we were good friends, it came and went. Hopie was mostly my baby sister so I didn't have the same kind of relationship with her when we were small. But she was quite the little monkey."

As for her relationship with her parents when she was young, "We never had much of a relationship with Daddy because he was either at work, going in early and coming back late, or he played golf at the weekends, and he had lots of drinking and cocktail parties. During Prohibition he made something called 'tiger's milk' – a very potent something or other! My parents also used to go up to Canada to get bootleg liquor.

"When we went up to Gilmanton, New Hampshire in summer, we'd see him a bit more; he would take some vacation time, but otherwise it was weekends. He took the train up Friday night and went back Sunday night." It must be added, however, that while he was working and alone in New York in the summers, he sent Beverly postcards frequently during the week to keep in touch. They usually had funny pictures on them, or were sent as from the dog or cat to say how they missed her, or asked about her swimming progress and such. There still exists a bundle of these cards from the summer of 1921, when Bev was just three, which seem to have been sent almost every day. They are very sweet and caring and indicate a loving relationship. When Bev got a bit older she wrote cards back to her Dad often. These also seem to indicate a much faster postal delivery service than we enjoy today.

"We were much closer to Mother, and we saw more of her. She found it difficult because she was trying to be like some of the other fancy ladies around, and she took French lessons and bridge lessons and things. I think she did those things to 'keep up with the Jones', but she was really more of a homebody.

"I remember one famous thing that made quite an impression on her. I was sick in bed with something, and she came in wearing a blue and white checked simple cotton dress which I can picture to this day. I said to her 'I'm so glad you are wearing that dress, that means you will be home today.'

"We did have servants – we had a laundress who came to do the laundry. We had a gardener who came and did the yard and the garden. As well as Rosline, we had a young Irish girl named Helen who waited on the table – I think she must have lived somewhere else. But she'd go to Gilmanton for the summer with us, as would Kay."

CHAPTER 2

Gilmanton, New Hampshire

One very important aspect of life for the Kitchen family was their summers in Gilmanton, New Hampshire. The Kitchen family had been summering in Gilmanton since the 1870s when Vic's grandparents, Ziba and Maria Kitchen visited, and later built a house there. Eventually several houses in the town were owned by relatives. Today one of Beverly's nieces lives in Gilmanton and another has a summer house there, so the tradition continues.

Every year the Kitchens traveled to this lovely little town in the rolling hills of southern New Hampshire for the entire summer. Certainly Beverly went there starting the summer she turned one, and then every summer right up through her early twenties as well as many more times later in her life. Many of the family photos of that era were taken in Gilmanton, where scenes of blueberry picking, hikes up various hills and mountains, and swimming and boating on Loon Pond depict the good times had by all.

Beverly recalls, "Swimming in the pond was a big thing. In Loon Pond you automatically pulled leeches off you when you came out of the water because there were so many – it was just routine, you just pulled them off. I gather there aren't so many of them any more.

"Every summer we always sailed on Lake Winnepesaukee in the big steamer, the *Mount Washington*. We went to Lost River where we scrambled on rocks and in the caves. We always climbed Peaked Hill at least once every summer, and we had other hikes we did too.

"Beyond Grandma and Grandpa's big red house up the hill, there was a long rock where you could sit and watch the sunset, behind the pine woods."

Vic Kitchen in Gilmanton with Beverly and baby Myra, 1922

Beverly enjoying the waters of Loon Pond

Explaining why her grandfather (Joseph Moses Ward Kitchen) acquired more land in Gilmanton, Beverly responded, "Grandpa, who kept buying property, was a medical doctor and expert on tuberculosis (TB) and wrote a book on the subject. He bought the land because high, clean air was good for TB."

That was true, but there was more to her grandfather's story. Dr. Kitchen had been working on improving the quality of milk for the general public for decades, and was a leader, perhaps even a crusader, in the effort to raise the standards for purer, safer dairy production. He had bought a 500 acre farm in Gilmanton, called Robinswood Farm, where he kept a herd of cattle, and for 35 years did experiments and modeled how to produce, bottle, and sell milk safely. He also invented many things related to this field – such as a better machine for heating milk to pasteurize it, a machine to safely and firmly seal milk bottle tops and so on. He did have a deep concern about tuberculosis, and this was related to his dairy work, as TB was in those days frequently transmitted via unpasteurized milk.

"My Grandfather Kitchen was a friend of Thomas Edison back home in New Jersey, and they worked out some inventions together. He invented a few odd things including an exercising chair and a new improved type of toilet paper. We have the patent papers for those two things." In fact, Dr. Kitchen held over 20 patents for a wide variety of things, from the dairy related, to methods for economizing on heating fuel, to a better pot for growing orchids. Bev continued, "Grandpa grew orchids at his home in East Orange, NJ, and his wife, Myra Constant, was called on to paint pictures of them when they were in their prime. Dozens of these beautiful paintings are now owned by their descendants. Their house was on a hill overlooking the athletic fields of the high school so we could look out their back windows and see the football games being played."

Bev knew her Kitchen grandparents very well. She says, "Grandpa died when I was in high school, and I remember being jealous because my cousin Dick Lippincott went to the funeral but I wasn't considered old enough. I was thirteen then.

"Grandma Kitchen was an absolute dear – we all adored her. Aunt Minnie she was called." There are delightful photos of Minnie playing on the grass with her grandchildren and assorted pets.

"My father's sister, Mary Lippincott, and her family, including my cousins Dick, Bruce, and Don, were always around in summer too. There was quite a gang of us. There were Gilmans (as in <u>Gilman</u>ton) there long before, and there still are. Going to the pond was great. Grandpa Kitchen had bought part of the shoreline of the pond, so it was in our family and was the Loon Pond

Association. We loved to go down there for picnics and cookouts and sometimes spend the night, and swim of course." Today it is called the Loon Lake Beach Corporation and has a number of active families who are members, including Bev's two nieces with homes there. There have now been seven generations of the family that have swum in those waters, and everyone gets to the pond by driving down Kitchen Lane.

Vic and Elsie Kitchen owned a house called Inglesante in Gilmanton for many years, and that's where they stayed when they went there, summer or winter, sometimes spending Christmas there. Bev remembers one time when she and Hopie drove up from Boston (likely 1938-39) in deep winter and the car got stuck when it slid off the road, probably Allens Mills Rd. Soon, a truck came along with some local young men they knew who gallantly lifted the car back onto the road again. Bev also remembers driving the car across Rocky Pond when it was frozen over, and slamming on the brakes to skid around! "That was great fun," she says.

Two other features of Gilmanton life that merit mention are the outhouse and the Lighthouse. The outhouse dated from when the Inglesante property was, long ago, part of a summer camp and had an "eleven-holer" for toileting use, divided between the men's and women's sides. Beverly remembers using it when she was a girl, though not very happily. It seems to have finally been removed in the 1970s.

The Lighthouse was the name for the big room at the back of Inglesante, used for parties and indoor fun on rainy days. It was called this because at both ends of the room were large mural paintings of lighthouses – inspired by the lighthouse logo for Vic Kitchen's advertising company. One of the paintings was destroyed in a storm that broke the roof, but the other one was moved to Bev's niece Wendy Berlind's home in Gilmanton where it adorns their big room, similarly used now for family fun and gatherings.

CHAPTER 3

Changes

Although life seemed to be generally good for the Kitchens, and the girls seem to have had a happy comfortable childhood, there was also some dissatisfaction and stress. Victor shared his personal journey in the book, *I Was A Pagan*, published in 1934 when Beverly was sixteen. In it he tells of the questioning and struggles in life he was facing by the early 1930s. Although a partner in his advertising company, he was not happy in his work; he was seeking to find meaning in his life, he was drinking too much, and seems to have not been very satisfied at home or in his marriage either. Perhaps from Bev's mention earlier of her mother "trying to keep up with the Jones", Elsie was also feeling these strains and unhappiness. Whatever the reasons, Victor and Elsie were not very happy in this period, and he at least was searching for something more meaningful.

In recollections written by Victor in 1963 he says more about this time in his life. Vic's mother was a woman of deep faith who had dedicated her son to God when he was born. It had been deeply painful for her when her own brother became an alcoholic. "It was my mother's dismay about her brother that sent her into the Women's Christian Temperance Union, and which thus caused her such distress when I seemed to be following in my uncle's booze footsteps." Vic also reflected on his marriage that, ". . . after 17 years of being buffeted around, if we had not learned to find steerage way under God's direction, our craft probably would have foundered. And under my daily alcoholic dosage I doubt that I would have lived beyond the age of 50."

Victor Kitchen in his advertising office

Around 1931, Victor met a group of people called the Oxford Group (OG) through which he did begin to find new meaning to life, a faith, and also a fresh partnership with his wife. Although his mother had given him to God as a baby, he says, "It wasn't until I was 40 years old, on 9 April 1932, that the gift from my part was voluntarily completed. As Elsie and I surrendered together, we look on this as our joint Spiritual Birthday." For them that meant seeking God's leading for their lives and putting things right where they could. For more information on the Oxford Group and its successor, Moral Re-Armament, please see the Appendix.

To thirteen year-old Beverly and her sisters, one early practical outcome of this was that Vic finally agreed to buy the family a dog, for which the girls had been asking for years! The dog was named Briarcliff, after Briarcliff Manor, NY where Victor had gone to his first Oxford Group house party.

Many things changed for the Kitchen family after this encounter. Victor stopped drinking and was in fact one of the early pioneers of Alcoholics Anonymous (AA) and their 12-step program.[1] He and Elsie became very involved in the Oxford Group and hosted people in their home as well as going to meetings of the Group.

One amusing note: after Vic's book, *I Was a Pagan*, came out, the Kitchens' maid overheard some conversation about it. Unfamiliar with the word *pagan*, she thought he'd called himself a pigeon, was quite mystified and asked for an explanation. The story spread, however, and Victor thus earned the nickname 'Pidge', which was used for many years by family and friends.

Apparently, despite the purchase of the dog, the girls were not entirely thrilled by all aspects of this new life style. One sign of this was clearly shown one evening when OG guests were coming to stay, and Beverly (then about 14) was expected to let these guests use her room, and she had to "go across the hall and share a room with my dear sister, Myra, and I was not happy about it. They went out to dinner or a meeting or something, so I just removed all the guests' belongings, clothes and everything out into the hall, and I went back into my own room. So when they came back late at night, ready to go to bed . . . I can't remember what happened, but I was not very popular!"

---

1 More about Vic's AA history is told in the book, *Changed By Grace: Vic Kitchen, The Oxford Group and AA* - by Glenn F. Chesnut (2006).

The Kitchens' new involvement, although profound and transformational for them, wasn't entirely popular with others in the family either. Both Bev and her cousin Betsy Wilson (daughter of Elsie's youngest sister, Ginny) remember that some of the Rodmans were upset about the new ideas and resented time taken away from family because of OG ideas or programs. Some were especially irked by Vic's refusal to drink any more – even going to the lengths of holding him down and trying to pour drinks down his throat to change his mind!

By 1934, Vic and Elsie decided that they should work on a full-time basis with the Oxford Group, and decided to sell their home in Great Neck in order to be available to travel as needed. They would continue to work with the OG and its successor Moral Re-Armament (MRA) for much of the rest of their lives.

Although they still had Inglesante in Gilmanton as a home base, the girls were all sent to boarding schools at this time. Hope (aged nine) was sent to a school in Mt. Kisco, New York; and Beverly and Myra were sent off to another school in Birmingham, Pennsylvania – chosen because of an Oxford Group connection the Kitchens had with the headmaster's wife, Mrs. Moulton. That school had originally been called The Mountain Female Seminary, was renamed the Birmingham School for Girls (the name when Bev and Myra were there), and is still going today as The Grier School. "So it was worked out that my sister Myra and I would go there. Because of the OG association, for which we had no use, we thought we were being sent to 'a religious dump in the mountains.' In fact it turned out that others in the school were not of the same persuasion, specifically Mr. Moulton, the headmaster, whom we called 'Pop' Moulton. He was not an advocate of the OG, nor anything, as I remember, nor terribly religious.

"As far as Myra and I were concerned, when we were sent off to the boarding school, it was the two of us against the world; we really became friends then. But in fact, we enjoyed it very much, and made lifelong friends. One of my roommates was Virginia (Ginny) Thornburg, whose 'baby' brother Richard later became Governor of Pennsylvania and then Attorney General of the USA. I was a bridesmaid at Ginny's wedding when Dick was 'little Dickie'. Her sister Anne and I shared an apartment for a time in NYC years later when we were both working there. Anne and I saw each other from time to time, because she lived in NYC for a long time.

" I know some of my other friends and roommates from there have died. One of them was Betty Ribble who later became a Powers Model. She was famous for putting ketchup on everything, including ice cream. She was tall, blonde and very beautiful.

Beverly in her senior year

"In our senior year, Ginny Thornburg, Jean Richardson and I had a suite with a big double bed-room and a single bedroom. We put all three beds in the double bedroom and all three desks in the single bed-room so we could study if we want-ed, or sleep. And Jean, I think it was, had smuggled into school, thorough-ly illegally, one of those flat things you toast sandwiches on, an electric grill – so we used to have toasted cheese sandwiches. We hid it in the closet, and I don't think it was ever found. Just across the hall from our suite was Miss Thompson, the gym teacher and hall proctor, and we made her life miserable. (We never understood why she didn't smell our toasting sandwiches.) She was a timid little mouse, just not our favorite person. One night Ginny and I decided we would do something. We had a metal scrap basket which we put under Jean's bed, with a spool of thread in it. The spool of thread was pulled out, so after we had gotten in bed and we were sort of half asleep, one of us would pull on the thread and this spool of thread would rattle in the waste basket. Since Jean was terrified of mice, of course she 'knew' it was a mouse, and there was a great deal of consternation. So in comes Miss Thompson, turns on the light and grabs a hockey stick to go after the mouse. Ginny and I were laughing so hard we really were not much help. She never found the mouse!

"That senior year, Ginny was head of student council by then, so it made life a little difficult for us as we did things she wasn't supposed to approve of. One night we worked up a prank we had heard of at another school. It started at one end of one corridor and went all the way down one side, down the other side, down a floor and the same thing there – everyone slamming their doors, so every single door got slammed in succession – bang, bang, bang … all the way through the whole school. We got everybody in the whole school to do it. We planned it thoroughly. There might have been some 'pantywaists' who didn't take part, but it was very successful!

"I was not popular with the boys, and high school is when I started smoking, because I was so little and not attractive-looking, so boys were not at all interested. I thought smoking would make me look more sophisticated and more desirable. It didn't work.

"There was another teacher, Miss Pennyfeather, who was a favorite, or I was a favorite of hers, and we used to have boys' schools come over for dances. So one time she picked this very handsome lad and brought him over to introduce him to me, and after I started dancing with him I discovered he only had one ear. It was quite a shock, both to the teacher and to me!

"The whole school was divided into green and gold teams. I was a gold and my sister Myra was green, so we were arch enemies on that score. But I loved field hockey, and I think I must have played that in Great Neck High School too. The only sports letter

I ever got awarded was for field hockey, but I don't remember what position I played. I was too short for basketball, I was hopeless at that. There was a swimming pool there; and we had military drill, which had started during WWI. The uniforms for that were green jumpers with white blouses – long sleeved in winter, short in summer. We had wooden guns, and we learned how to march, how to present arms, right, left, and the whole military drill, literally, on the athletic field. There was also a white uniform we wore on Sundays or special days.

Beverly (front right) with field hockey teammates

"Our school was on a hill above the Juniata River, a branch of the Susquehanna River, and there was a paper mill upstream somewhere. And sometimes the stuff the paper mill would put out had the most disgusting smell, and it wafted up the hill and overwhelmed us at times.

"One time the river flooded badly, and we couldn't get out of the school because the road below was all flooded too, and I remember there were a lot of houses all along the river, very poor people. We went down there after the flooding, and it was heartbreaking to see those houses all full of guck. I think that's the first time I ever thought of big scale tragedy because I saw it right there.

"I remember one time we were driving to school with mother and a pheasant flew up and was killed by hitting the front of the windshield. We picked it up and took it to the school, and I think someone cooked it, but I don't think we ever got any.

"I went riding there. I think that's the first time I ever went riding. I never particularly liked it, and I got thrown off a horse more than once. I was never a good rider."

About ten letters written by Bev from the Birmingham School survive and are delightful to read all these years later. Her strong skills as a letter writer were already apparent, and most of her letters were lengthy. Included are lots of school news, activities, hockey, performances, etc., as well as many requests for more money and various items she wants sent from home. There are also sprinklings of French words and phrases included as she practiced her new language skills.

Beverly spent her junior and senior years at the Birmingham School and graduated in 1936. Her sister Myra attended for two more years. In retrospect, Beverly is rather puzzled and amused at the negative feelings they seem to have had before going to the school, because they both enjoyed and benefited from it in the end.

Right at the time of Beverly's graduation, there was a huge Oxford Group house-party with about five thousand people going on in Stockbridge, Massachusetts (MA), called "America Awake". "Mother and Daddy and Hope were at that. My mother came from Stockbridge for my graduation and picked us up and took us back there." Not only were there many people at this gathering, but it received wide coverage in the press. A reporter for the *New York Times* was sending in daily reports from the house-party for almost two weeks, and there were also regular reports in national newsreels.

"A Vassar College student called Eleanor Morris was assigned to care for me, and she became a life-long friend. She had a great sense of humor. I smoked a lot, trying to shock the OG people, but I didn't shock Eleanor – she was great, she really was good. I wasn't very helpful.

"That house-party was based at the Red Lion Inn in Stockbridge, MA, and I don't know where my parents, Myra, or Hope were living, but I was staying in Jug End Barn in South Egremont, Massachusetts. Little did I know I would end up living in Egremont all these years later."

This assembly went on for almost two weeks, and because there were so many people there and they didn't have motels then – people stayed at inns and cottages, and in private homes. Beverly has met people around Egremont in recent years who remember their parents taking attendees into their homes at that time.

"So when the house-party was over, we went to Gilmanton for the summer, to our home of Inglesante, as we did every summer for as long as we could remember. At different times various OG people came there to visit. One was H.W. 'Bunny' Austin, the British tennis champion in the 1930s, who played on our tennis court. I also remember the visit of Ruth Devienne, later Kennedy, who remained a life-long friend."

CHAPTER 4

Working Girl

During that summer of 1936, after high school, Beverly was naturally looking at her future and trying to decide what to do with her life. "I wanted to do something medical, and feeling that I was too slap-dash to be trusted with people's lives as a nurse or a doctor, I settled for a medical secretary. I tried to get into the junior college in New London, New Hampshire, which had an excellent two year course where you learned basic lab techniques and secretarial training, but they had a two year waiting list. So I settled on Miss Pierce's Secretarial School on Boylston St. in Boston."

At that time, Victor and Elsie were living with Hopie in a house in Cambridge, MA along with two other couples, Lee and Helen Vrooman, and Ed and Gwen Perry, together creating a kind of center or meeting place for Oxford Group people. Beverly recalls that they then moved to Brookline, MA which is where she joined them.

"At this point, I was living with Mother and Daddy and Hopie, in half a house in Brookline, and the landlady, Mrs. Hayes, a delightful lady, lived in the other half." A story about sister Hope from this time shows her independent spirit. She was about twelve years old and totally vanished one day, to the great consternation of all the family. When she eventually returned home, she told them that she and a friend had decided to go see a movie starring their idol in Boston and enjoyed it so much they stayed and watched it twice. But they had not told anyone where they were going in the first place!

Beverly continues, "After a year at secretarial school, I then joined the Palmer Memorial Hospital to work in their record room. There was a staff of four: Miss Studley (the boss), Evelyn Wilson (another older maiden lady), a third woman, nearer my age, and myself, the junior one. We all became good friends.

"Since I knew no medical terminology, I was sat down with a dictaphone (I think that's what you called it). You had these wax cylinders and you had two pedals and earphones. You'd press one pedal and the cylinder would start going around and you'd hear the words of the dictation and you'd type it. When you came across a word you didn't know, you'd take your foot off the pedal and push the back pedal and listen again, and go back and forth and listen and listen. Then you'd get out the medical dictionary and find the closest thing you could to what you thought they'd said. Sometimes it was absolutely bizarre, because I thought I'd found the word and it was, say, the left toe, and then it would turn out to be an inner ear infection or something! The interns who dictated the case histories and records got big kicks out of that.

"There was one guy, an intern, who I really liked, T. Hugh Lee. I'd be listening to his dictation about a really serious matter, typing along, and then suddenly out would come something from Winnie the Pooh. I'd be typing on a bit before I'd realize what he had done to tease me. He was rather a nice guy, I did a couple of things with him, and we went on a couple of dates.

"Then they would have clinics, and I'd sit in on those, and the doctors would dictate whatever they wanted about the people they examined. I also took dictation while they read x-rays. I loved going up to the operating room and sometimes could go in and actually watch what they were doing. If they were doing something not routine, they wanted to have special clear notes on it."

When asked if that ever made her queasy or seemed gory, Bev replied, " No, that was OK, but I didn't want to go downstairs and have cold macaroni salad in the cafeteria after watching surgery!"

Palmer Memorial Hospital was primarily for cancer care, and it was a part of the New England Deaconess Hospital. In later years, NEDH grew as a hospital with various specialty units, and then in 1996 merged with Beth Israel, a more general hospital that had been NEDH's neighbor for 50 years, to form Beth Israel Deaconess Medical Center. "NEDH, right next to us in Palmer, was where Dr. Joslin, the diabetes expert, hung out with his crew. He was world-famous and had at least one son I knew who worked with him. Then there was Dr. Priscilla White, a wonderful woman. [2] They had quite a staff there, and did amazing work.

"I remember talking to one of the nurses one time, and I said 'I don't know how you do what you're doing, with people dying and so on.' She said, 'You either have to have a heart of stone and close your heart and do your job, or you have to have a very strong faith.' I'll never forget that."

Soon after Bev started working in Boston she used some of her early earnings to buy a used car which had a canvas top and a rumble seat, and was christened "Baby". This car was happily used during her Boston years, for travels around town, in the suburbs and sometimes to go to Gilmanton.

As well as her work at the hospital, Beverly seems to have had an active social and cultural life in Boston. Her scrapbook of this period is filled with programs for a wide range of concerts,

2 Dr. White joined Dr. Joslin at NEDH when she was just 24, in 1924, and by the late 1930s was doing pioneering work on gestational diabetes and the importance of monitoring blood glucose during pregnancy

plays, and meetings. She was a regular attender at the Boston Pops concerts and heard famous musicians such as Horowitz, Sergei Rachmaninoff, and Jan Smeterlin at Symphony Hall and Jordan Hall. She also attended political and community events, heard prominent federal prosecutor Thomas Dewey speak, and was at a Foreign Policy Association meeting in Feb.1940 where the pros and cons of neutrality were debated. And tucked into the back of her scrapbook is a suggested reading list of books on "Europe in Crisis" – all signs of an active and seeking mind.

Interestingly, one other aspect of Bev's lifelong search for adventure is shown by a letter from the U.S. Dept. of the Interior in May, 1940, regretting to inform her, in response to her inquiry, that there were no job openings available for her in Alaska at that time.

"I think I worked at Palmer Memorial for about three years. For the first two Mother and Daddy and Hopie were in Brookline, and I stayed with them; and then they moved to West Orange, New Jersey. Myra was still at The Birmingham School two more years, until 1938 when she graduated and then she started at Vassar College. Beverly commented "She was a natural scholar and got very good grades, unlike me.

"When my parents and Hopie left Boston for New Jersey, I went to stay with the Street family. Mrs. Mary Street was a widow and had two daughters about my age, and she took in one or two other people as boarders. That was fun. They were a good family and we enjoyed each other. Mrs. Street had some connection with the Oxford Group, and Mother knew her, but she wasn't deeply involved.

"After a year with the Streets, I decided to leave Boston and go live with my family in New Jersey. So in the summer of 1940 I moved in with Mother, Daddy and Hopie at their house in West Orange. That summer was a busy one for our family. Mother and Daddy were somewhere with the OG part of the time, so I took care of Hopie, who was a teenager in high school there, Miss Beard's School. It was Mother and Daddy's 25th wedding anniversary in June; and that same month Myra got married to Bill Prindle, whom she had met through his sister, Fran, a friend of her's at Vassar College. They were married from Ginny and Bus Reed's house in near-by Short Hills, New Jersey, as our house was too small."

The Kitchens on Vic and Elsie's 25th anniversary, June 1940

It is interesting to note that Beverly, although saying she was not at all interested in the Oxford Group, still chose to come back to live with her family, who were deeply involved in it. It should be noted here that in 1938 the Oxford Group changed its name to Moral Re- Armament (MRA).

Beverly recalls a conversation with her father one day when he was trying to tell her why the ideas of MRA would be helpful to her. She just told him "I don't need that, I'm perfectly happy without it." His response? "But what about your friend Jean? Could you help her?" Jean was an old friend who was going through a hard time, which Vic knew about. Although Bev was struck by his point, to the extent that that conversation is still clear in her mind many decades later, she still didn't feel MRA was for her.

Bev continues her story. "I tried around New Jersey for a job in the fall of 1940 and got nowhere, and that's when I got a job with the R.H. Macy Company (the original Macy's department store) right in New York City. That meant that I had to get up at 6:30 am to get the train in from NJ to work in the city. I was working at Macy's in-store clinic on the 19th floor, and was the secretary to the Medical Director, Dr. Michael Lake, a very nice guy. There was a staff of 15-20 people there and they had a laboratory and an x-ray machine, but no overnight patients or operating room. There were hundreds of employees who worked in the store and warehouses, and anyone who was going to be employed there had to have a physical. They were all supposed to have an annual check-up, but that didn't always work out as there were too many people. If you were out sick, you had to come and check back in at the clinic. If you needed injections or tests, or if you felt sick, or had an injury on the job, you would come there."

One funny experience Bev had while at Macy's occurred when a maintenance man at the store accidentally hit a fire sprinkler on the ceiling with a ladder while carrying it on an escalator. Many shoppers got very wet, and they were all brought to the clinic to sit wrapped in blankets while their clothes were dried!

Beverly made some new friends while working at Macy's; Grace Ahern and Billie, who were both nurses in the Macy's hospital, and who lived in Queens, NYC. "Sometimes if we were going to do something in the evening, I'd go home with them, rather than go back out to NJ. We were good friends and remained so for years.

Billie married her boyfriend, Ray de Martino, and they were a re-ally nice pair, and later moved south somewhere. We kept in touch for a long time, and they sent me a small painting Ray had done in 2003. Grace we saw in New York in the 1970s, but she has long since died. They were both a bit older than me, and both very tall, and I am very short, so we were a funny combination."

Ready to make a splash in the big city

Not surprisingly for a lively young lady in her early 20s, she also had some romantic adventures while in New York. There was one fellow, whose name is now forgotten, who she dated for a time. He was a medical student, so that made him interesting to her. He actually donated blood somewhere, got paid for it, and then used that money to buy Beverly an engagement ring, to her great surprise. But she says, "One time we had gone together to Gilmanton in the summer when all the gang was there, and when I saw him in the context of all our family and friends, I just knew it wasn't going to work. So that's when we broke that one off. He just didn't seem comfortable there." Beverly then chuckled and added, "Oh I gave my parents some scares along the way! There was somebody else once too. I had gone somewhere with Mother and Daddy for a weekend, and he called up – he was a disaster! Probably some of these things are best forgotten!"

Beverly was also, thanks to her aunt Ginny Reed, a member of the Junior League, an organization of women who did volunteer work of many kinds to help those less fortunate than themselves. She worked as a volunteer in a clinic in New York.

In Dec. 1941, Pearl Harbor was bombed, and the USA joined in WWII. Some time after that Dr. Lake left Macy's to join the Navy, and Beverly didn't really like the man who took his place. Her only memory of hearing about the Pearl Harbor attack is that she was in New Jersey, and remembers thinking about it with shock as she walked along a street. It was such a complete surprise.

One final note about Macy's in the war time: Beverly had a window box on that 19ᵗʰ floor that was a Victory Garden. In it she grew portulaca and carrots. She claims to have liked portulaca ever since because they grew so well, but wasn't sure that she produced many carrots.

CHAPTER 5

The War – Washington

"**A**t some point I decided I wanted to do something for the war effort, and so I went to Washington. I was really hoping to get a job that would take me overseas. I stayed for quite a while with the Cutlers – 'Aunt' Polly and 'Uncle' Sam Cutler and their daughter Polly (about my age) who were old family friends from Gilmanton. They had a big apartment in Washington.

"Polly later joined the WASPs (Women Airforce Service Pilots, started in 1942) who flew planes around the country to test them and to deliver them to the Air Force." There were over 1,100 women who did this with little recognition of any kind for almost 70 years. Then in 2010 their service was finally celebrated in Washington, DC to recognize their extraordinary contribution to the war effort. Beverly is still in touch with Polly, who sent her an article about this event.

Bev continues, "I found a job with the Red Cross, thinking that would get me overseas, but it didn't and that job was a complete disaster, very boring. My Aunt Ginny and Uncle Bus Reed were by then living in Falls Church, Virginia, and Bus was working in military intelligence. Knowing how very unhappy I was with the Red

Cross, he said 'Would you like to come and work at the Pentagon?', and I said 'Sure, I'll try it'. Bus was a personnel man, and he said to Colonel Carter Clarke, who was in charge of the Special Branch of Military Intelligence, 'I can't hire this girl. She's my niece, you talk to her.' So I was left in the room with Col. Clarke to be interviewed, and I was hired." This was in the summer of 1942.

Although it was true that Bev's uncle couldn't hire her himself, he could vouch for her background and security. This was a very important factor in that while Intelligence needed to be sure of who they hired, they also needed people quickly, and a full FBI background check would have taken six months. So this was a crash program to get people into Military Intelligence. One could say that nepotism was useful here! In fact, there were several people in that Military Intelligence office who had been at the law firm Bus Reed had worked at in New York, all brought into the Pentagon in the same way. At a desk near Bev's, for example, was Betsy (later Mrs. Gordon Stott), daughter of Bus's partner from his law firm. According to Bev, "She was a slightly higher echelon than I was due to her college education. We became friends then and remained so for years.

"Col. Clarke worked across the hall in his big office, and I worked in Special Branch, in a big office with lots of desks, with officers and secretaries and evaluators, and an armed guard at the door. Charlie Paradise, who was a guy with a heart of gold, ran the secretaries' part of the office like a kindly drill sergeant. It's interesting, because years later when I read a story of Katherine Graham, she said he had been working at *The Washington Post* and was so valuable that he was greatly missed when he left to go into the intelligence service. Al Friendly, who had also worked at *The Washington Post*, came into Intelligence as well, and he was one of the officers in that office."

It is interesting that Intelligence needed engineers, lawyers, and all sorts of people, and they gave them some kind of rank to make it official, but none had had officer training, so they rather dispensed with protocol and rank in this branch.

Beverly continues her story; "I had been working at the Pentagon for a while already when Telford Taylor, one of the officers there, was going to Britain to start a group of Americans to work with the British, and he needed a secretary. No one else seemed to want it, and I was eager, so I got it!"

It's not really surprising that no one else wanted to go work in Britain in the middle of the bombing blitz in a war zone. Not to mention the grave dangers involved in crossing the Atlantic during wartime, especially in 1943 which had the worst number of Allied maritime losses, 95 ships lost in March of that year alone. It says a lot about this woman that despite all this possible danger, she still leapt at the chance to serve her country in this way.

Bev then had to wait for her official orders for travel to come through, and her excitement about being given this rather risky job in the war zone comes through clearly, as she wrote in her scrapbook on Sept. 22nd, 1943, "Colonel McCormack told me I <u>could</u> go to England! After dashing down to the dispensary and getting shots for typhus, typhoid, smallpox, and tetanus, I dropped what was left of the body on a train to St. Petersburg, Florida and went merrily on my way to spend my vacation with my sister Myra, her husband Bill, and their little son Pete, my godson." This was a welcome pre-travel break where Bev enjoyed the beach and some relaxed family time. Bill Prindle was working with the Coast Guard and continued to do so for many years in various locations on the east coast of the USA.

Meanwhile, Bev's sister Hope had graduated from the Beard School in June of 1943, and she and their parents were all working with MRA full-time, traveling around the country with various plays, including *The Forgotten Factor* and the *Drugstore Revolution*. They were also helping to run the MRA summer conferences on

Mackinac Island, Michigan, which began in 1942 and continued into the 1960s. Vic was also acting, writing, and doing publicity with MRA, and published a little booklet called "Time Bombs", filled with pithy sayings and good advice. One classic example: "If your children turn out to be bad eggs, maybe it's because you sat on them too long."

On October 19th, Beverly got her official travel orders (destination XXX'ed out), including the amount she would be paid for travel allowance and the amount of baggage she could take. At the top of this document, taped into her scrapbook, Bev has written, "I still don't believe it!" She had to wait a bit longer, however, as no specific date or mode of transport had yet been given, so she was able to spend that Thanksgiving with family. Then suddenly on Nov. 29th she was informed she would be leaving Washington, DC by train on Dec. 1st – so it was a mad dash to get herself finally ready. The one specific item she remembers taking was a gray flannel suit which she wore almost daily for months to come.

Thus, on Dec. 1st, 1943, Beverly and others also bound for government work in England, left Washington, DC by train for Philadelphia. The ticket stub for this 'Stage One' of her journey is in the scrapbook, along with a note saying, "We all had a steak dinner at Bookbinder's (a famous old restaurant in Philly) to celebrate our last night in the USA."

CHAPTER 6

An Unforgettable Voyage

The next day, Dec. 2nd, they set sail out of Philadelphia. Their ship, the *Joao Belo*, was Portuguese and was expected to be safer as Portugal was neutral in the war. Beverly was sharing a cabin with Marie Keohane, one of a group of eight young women going to work as civilians for the American government in England, most of them heading to the US Embassy in London. Bev describes this group by saying they "were variously taken for a show troupe or a girls' boarding school on tour!" In fact, all of those on board were either government people or missionaries.

The first day out, while still in the Delaware River, Bev and two others wanted to play ping-pong, but needed a fourth person. Bev spotted a tall young man walking along and thought she'd heard someone call him Harry. She recalls: "So I looked off in the other direction and said 'Harry', and he answered, so I asked if he would like to play ping pong. And the rest, as they say, is history!" They seem to have hit it off very quickly, and apparently began spending lots of time together walking around the deck – during which time Harry taught Bev the words to (inexplicably) "Waltzing Matilda", which they then sang together as they walked. They must have made quite a delightful-looking duo on these walks as Harry was a lanky 6' 2" with light brown hair and glasses, and Beverly a full foot shorter at 5' 2", with auburn/brown wavy hair.

Meanwhile, Marie, Bev's roommate, had rather fallen for Alberto, the Portuguese Assistant Purser on the ship. The four of them spent several evenings in Alberto's stateroom, sitting on the lower bunk with their feet up on the opposite wall, enjoying food and drink that Alberto could easily provide. An interesting time was apparently had by all, especially as Marie and Alberto had no common language; however Alberto spoke French, and Harry and Bev spoke a little – so translation was part of the courtship of these two romantic pairs.

The trip was not all romance, however, as it was war time and precautions were needed and taken. The neutral ship with its Portuguese flag painted on the sides was clearly flood-lit at night. It was a chilly voyage as the ship was equipped for the tropics, not the North Atlantic in December, so everyone wore their warmest things, and laid their coats on their beds at night.

In Harry Almond's memoir he recalls an episode from this trip. "One night during our voyage to the Azores, our first port of call, an unlit ship loomed up out of the dark, silhouetted by gunfire and torpedo flashes in the distance. We diverted due south by 100 miles before resuming our course."

He continues: "From Philadelphia it took ten days to reach the harbor of Ponta Delgada in the Azores. The seas calmed as we entered the anchorage, and the sunny skies and pastel-colored homes were a welcome relief after the heaving gray Atlantic.

"Just before arriving in the Azores I proposed to Beverly. We had been drinking, and her response was not very clear to either of us, but in the cold, clear light of morning we agreed she had said

'Yes!' I had only my high school class ring to give her, but she wore it happily, and still does."

Beverly soon wrote her family, saying to them, "There was a boy on board (Harry J. Almond by name) who turned out to be 'the most wonderful guy in the world!!!!' "

Harry J. Almond was a seminary student from New Jersey, en route to work for the Reformed Church of America as a short-term missionary teacher in Iraq. His story, as written by him in the book *An American in the Middle East*, tells much more of his background, but suffice it to say that he had been a pacifist until Pearl Harbor, then tried to enlist and was turned down due to less than perfect eyesight. He decided instead to take this teaching post as preparation for finishing seminary and then becoming a full missionary himself. He was on the *Joao Belo* as the start of his journey to Iraq; and traveling with Dr. and Mrs. John Van Ess – Dr. Van Ess being head of the Iraq mission, a linguist and Arabic scholar, and mentor to Harry.

Some years later, John Van Ess wrote a poem for the Almonds which recounts the meeting of Harry and Beverly. It goes in part like this:

> At last when the weather had cleared just a bit
> Came Harry from out second class,
> To talk of the future in store for him
> And whatever might come to pass.

> Now Harry was feeling ascetic you know,
> Austere is the word I prefer,
> He'd show any girl who might happen his way
> That in him there was nothing for her.
> Come to pass, did I say? The second day out

Passed a girl dressed in slacks very trim,
With bright auburn hair and a sweet winning smile
And a look manifestly for him.

The monk in our Harry he died on the spot,
Though he covered the corpse carefully,
For her eyes had said "ta'al"*, and he ta'aled right away
The captive of our Beverly.
(*ta'al means, in effect, 'come hither' in Arabic)

During the stop in the Azores lots of Portuguese military men got on, crowding the ship greatly, but none of the passengers could get off. They arrived in Lisbon a week later, on Dec. 19th, and disembarked there to prepare for the next stage in their travels.

Beverly was staying in one hotel with the other American women, and Harry was with the Van Esses at another not far away, so they quickly met up and decided they had to tell the Van Esses of their engagement. When Harry had been hired by the Reformed Church it was on the understanding that he was a single man without romantic commitments, but it was different now. In some fear and trepidation, he did tell them his news, and they were thrilled, and gave the young couple a celebratory dinner party that very evening. As it turned out, the Van Esses were very sympathetic in that they themselves had only known each other for about two weeks before getting engaged.

Beverly and Harry spent the next three days sight-seeing around Lisbon, doing needed shopping, and trying to get to know each other better and figure out their future. They managed to get an engagement photo taken, and also had tea at the American Embassy. In Bev's scrapbook is preserved the dried corsage that Harry managed to create and get delivered with the breakfast tray at her hotel one morning.

The engaged pair – taken in Lisbon, Dec. 21, 1943

When asked many decades later how she was feeling at that point, just engaged and about to part for an unknown period of time in the middle of the war, Beverly responded, "Pretty devastated, I think, but that was the war."

As the parting grew closer, it didn't help Harry to know that the very British airline flight 777-A that Bev was due to take had been attacked several times in the previous year by the Luftwaffe, and that just a few months earlier, in June, it had been attacked by eight German Junkers and crashed in the Bay of Biscay killing all on board, including actor Leslie Howard. Certainly the reality of the war came a lot closer for both of them at this point.

The time quickly came to say goodbye, and on the night of Dec. 22nd, Beverly took her flight for England, not to see her fiancé again for two and a half years. (Incidentally this was the first airplane flight she had ever been on.) She landed safely at Whitchurch Airport near Bristol and went by train up to London, a trip which she says in her scrapbook, "we'd rather forget." She and her group, still together, were sent to the Strand Palace Hotel, where she stayed for the next five days. She adds, "Of course this was the first experience we'd had with the blackout, and there was an air raid where we all came out in the hall, but didn't know what to do."

Nevertheless, during that short time, these American women somehow managed to see the Changing of the Guard at Buckingham Palace, Westminster Abbey, Big Ben, the Houses of Parliament, the Cenotaph, and Downing Street – making the most of their opportunity to be 'tourists' over the Christmas holidays before they started work.

Beverly had been given an introduction by her parents to MRA people in London, and amazingly, her cabin mate Marie had been given a similar introduction by a family friend, so they got in touch with those people and were invited to come and visit on Dec. 26th, known in England as Boxing Day. They thought that at least there would be some friendly faces and a pleasant setting to be in far from home at Christmas time.

Bev writes, "We spent Boxing Day afternoon at 4 Hays Mews (the address of the MRA center in London). Here we had our only taste of Christmas. There was a tree lit with real candles, and we all sat on the floor around it and were given Christmas presents of things we needed (mine was a coat hanger, as I had lamented my very slight association with same for many a month), and sang Christmas carols until the last candle burned out." Clearly this experience was a very special one for Beverly, far from home at Christmas, so much so that she kept the gift tag from her gift in her scrapbook. She talks about this visit in deeply grateful terms to this day – over 70 years later.

Beverly recalls the advice that was given to her at this time by her new boss, Lt. Colonel Telford Taylor: "You will have much to get used to – blackouts, buzz bombs, new people, places and experiences – and then it will be spring!" She held onto that advice and it helped her as she began her assignment.

In the scrapbook she wrote, "On Wednesday, 29th December, I was given orders and moved to the country. I am now on travel status, except when actually in London." The address she was given to receive mail was c/o Military Attaché, US Embassy, London. The Christmas letter the Kitchens sent out in Dec. 1943 said, "Beverly was sent to London, England to work for the Army", because that's all they knew.

Meanwhile, Harry continued his circuitous journey around the whole of Africa and then across the Middle East, not arriving in Basra, Iraq until March 15th, 115 days after leaving Philadelphia.

CHAPTER 7

Station X

I n fact Beverly had gone to work at Bletchley Park, an estate in
the countryside of Buckinghamshire, about 50 miles north of
London. This site was one of the most top-secret operations in
Britain, and incredibly vital to the war. Bletchley Park had been chosen in 1938 as a safe location outside London for intelligence services
to use and it was called Station X. Part of the reason for this choice
of location was that the town was at the intersection of two railroad
lines, one going quickly into London and the other running between
Oxford and Cambridge. As war neared and then began for Britain in
September 1939, operations grew rapidly, as did the number of those
working there. The primary focus was on intercepting and decoding
messages sent by those in the German military to each other.

In 1932, the Poles had gotten an encoding machine, called
Enigma, from the Germans when it was undergoing trials, and they
had broken the code then. At the time the Poles first did that, the
cipher altered only once every few months. With the advent of war,
however, it changed at least once a day, giving an almost inconceiv-
able 159 million, million, million possible settings to choose from!
The Poles decided to inform the British about this in July, 1939, since
they needed help to break the Enigma code, and with the German
invasion of Poland imminent. Bletchley Park became the center for

this operation, and as more and more people arrived to join the code-breaking operations, the various sections began to move into large pre-fabricated wooden huts set up on the lawns of the Park. For security reasons the various sections were known only by their hut numbers.

At the time of writing this book the film *The Imitation Game* had just come out, and so Bletchley Park, and especially Alan Turing, the famous cryptanalyst who is the film's main character, have become much more widely known. Beverly and other friends still alive from that time are glad the story is being told, but have some problems with the film's accuracy and the 'Hollywoodization' of the story. One such English friend, Pauline Burrough Lee, was invited to the premiere of the film in London as an honored guest. When she saw the shot depicting the main house at Bletchley, she couldn't help exclaiming out loud, "That's not right!" In fact she was quite correct, as none of the film was actually shot at Bletchley Park.

Bletchley Park – the main building
Photo taken in 1992 when the author visited there.
She and her son John are in the doorway.

The very first American to work long term at Bletchley was Joe Eachus, a physics professor who had taken up cryptanalysis as a hobby and was then recruited by the Navy. After showing Alan Turing around Washington when Turing visited the USA in 1942, Eachus found himself sent to Bletchley shortly afterwards, and thus became the first American of any service to go to there, not as a visitor or as a liason officer, but as a working cryptanalyst.

Another group of Americans, led by Army Signal Corps officer William (Bill) Bundy[3], began work in Hut 6 in August, 1943, and were a part of the code-breaking and translation operations.

Lt. Col. Telford Taylor was a lawyer and government prosecutor who had, when the US joined the war, worked at the Pentagon and then in the US Embassy in London in intelligence with Special Branch. He arrived at Bletchley Park in July of 1943 to set up the office in Hut 3 that would select and send information decoded from Enigma to Special Branch at the Pentagon. He was joined in August by his first staff person, Major Sam McKee, and the first of their messages was sent to Washington, DC on August 27th, 1943.

It is not the job of this book to explain all the workings of Bletchley Park or the significance of all that happened there. There are many excellent books that describe this amazing effort. One book in particular, *The Ultra Americans*, by Thomas Parrish, focuses on the backgrounds, activities, and adventures of the Americans at Bletchley – including Beverly Kitchen, who was interviewed for and contributed photos to that book. At the time the Americans began arriving, there were already about 5,000 people working there, but only 400-500 of them actually worked in Hut 6 (decoding)

---

3 William "Bill" Bundy (1917 – 2000), was later an attorney and intelligence expert, and an analyst with the CIA. He was notable as a foreign affairs advisor to both presidents John F. Kennedy and Lyndon B. Johnson.

and Hut 3 (transmission of information). In fact very few people at the Park even knew what was going on in those two huts.

This was the extraordinary place which Beverly came to at the very end of 1943 and where she worked for the next 22 months. It was vital that no one know about the site or what was going on there. They were all sworn to secrecy and understood how essential it was to reveal nothing about the operation to anyone. Certainly Bev took this promise very seriously indeed and did not breathe a word about it to anyone for over thirty years. She remembers one colleague there who had to have surgery and was terrified she would reveal something top secret while under the anesthetic. Churchill described those who worked at Bletchley Park as "The geese who laid the golden eggs, and never cackled."

Wonderfully, Beverly made a scrapbook about her time in England and kept lots of little souvenirs to share with her family after the war. She also wrote frequent letters to her family, multiple carbon copies for all the branches, many of which survive to fill in the story. What is most extraordinary is how she was able to write these regular lengthy epistles and yet never, ever mention what she was actually doing, or where she was. At least half of each letter seems to be a response to all the family news received, or detailed thanks for welcome goodies sent to her by relatives; treasures such as clothes, food, or even bobbie pins or candy. She writes about her French lessons, the knitting she had done, the weather, some sightseeing, how she managed to do her laundry and ironing, movies and shows she had seen, folks she visited, chatting with friends, having drinks, going for bike rides and so on. The closest she gets to referring to work is mention of such social events as " having tea with the wonderful wife of one of the men at work and her love of a three-year-old daughter," or a reference to "going back to the factory."

Upon arrival, Bev was billeted at the White Hart Hotel in Buckingham, the county town of Buckinghamshire about 10 miles from Bletchley Park. She wrote in her scrapbook, "I am indeed very lucky to be billeted at the White Hart Hotel – although my room is cold as hell, the ironing facilities are not exactly adequate, and we have brussels sprouts and golden pudding every night for dinner – the staff are wonderful, the food is delicious, my room is very comfortable (except for the temperature), and the other inhabitants are ever-changing and most interesting. The couple, Mr. and Mrs. Firth, who run the hotel are very nice people too." Her room was at the back, at the end of the hall, and overlooking the garden. She later added, "The only heat was a gas stove that you made work by putting money in it, shillings or something. So I would sit in front of that stove and be warm in front and freezing in the back." She was the only American staying there for some time, and certainly the only American young woman, so quite a novelty.

Happily, one of her fellow passengers on the *Joao Belo* had told her, "My dear, you simply can't exist in England without a hot water bottle. I'll give you one as soon as we get there." She made good on her promise, so at least in bed at night Bev could stay warm.

As most of the Bletchley staff were billeted with local families or in various inns and hotels around the area, every day a "shooting brake" (like a station wagon) would do its rounds and pick up those who were working at the Park, including Bev. One person met on that commute to work, who became a good friend and with whom she is still in touch – both of them now in their 90s (in 2015), was the afore-mentioned Pauline Burrough (Lee). She was also billeted in Buckingham, but in the cottage of an elderly policeman and his wife who treated her like their daughter.

The following is what Beverly remembers from those days about her work. "Our Special Branch office was one room in one of the huts (Hut 3-US). Telford was there and Sam McKee, and for one stretch – Ted Hilles, who had been an English professor at Yale. All the others came and went. They came and got training in what was going on at Bletchley and then would go out in the field and work with the generals or whoever were the recipients of the secret messages that came out from us to them. I would be typing up messages or letters or whatever. I think probably that Telford and the others who were responsible would get the whole message, and then they would take what they felt was needed out of it and then dictate it, and we'd send it off. I don't remember how we sent it off. We got fed the news that the code breakers produced, and that news was then sent to people in the field. Our office sent it to the Americans.

"The office had a couple of big tables, and maybe some smaller ones – about 5-6 people could work there at one time. It was very rudimentary, not fancy at all. We did have a couple of windows, but walls on three sides. It must have been heated, but I don't think we were overheated! I always wore my gray flannel suit; it was like my uniform that I wore most of the time – so that kept me warmer."

Lt. Col. Telford Taylor,
"The Boss", at his desk

Thomas Parrish, after interviewing Beverly in August 1984, wrote, in his book *The Ultra Americans*, "For some six months Beverly Kitchen, as the only woman and *a fortiori* the only secretarial person in 3-US, was incessantly busy taking dictation and producing translations, letters, and reports, none of which interested her in the slightest. 'There were Luftwaffes, SS's, and all this kind of stuff that I typed up by the yard, but I was so uninterested in it.' She was at Bletchley Park to be useful and to be part of an adventure, but in the most traditional fashion she thought of war as a man's game.

She worked for everyone in the office, though first of all she was Telford Taylor's secretary, and the volume of work, the flood of endless specific details about German military organizations, no doubt had a numbing effect on a mind that was sprightly but hardly military." As Bev actually worked at Bletchley for over twenty months, Parrish's mention of six months refers to the time before she was joined by another woman, Annabel Grover.

Beverly certainly did work very hard. She was collected each morning by the brake and stayed "until the work was done", sometimes well into the evening. A page in the scrapbook describing a weekend visit to the home of English friend Elizabeth Everard mentions that it was "my first two days off since I've been here". That was in mid-April, after over 3½ months at Bletchley. She did have occasional single days off and made the most of them – more on that later. Beverly soon got a bicycle and used that to get around in those rare times off.

As well as doing all the secretarial work for this office at Bletchley, as described above, Bev went to London about once a week for a day and worked for Capt. Lou Stone, "a great big guy", also of Special Branch, though as part of a group called TICOM. (The acronym stood for Target Identification Committee.) "We had an office in a block of offices in London, not in the embassy or anything because it was hush-hush – just in a regular office building," says Bev.

There is mention in Bev's scrapbook of a London visit in March of 1944 when she experienced "my first real air raid during which I balanced my checkbook and wrote letters". When asked how she just calmly did that, she replied, "What else?"

Regarding other air raid experiences; "I think I always stayed with Marie (Keohane, her cabin mate from the ship) when I was overnight in London. She worked at the Embassy. The only thing I remember was one time I was in London, I was taking a bath (it was daylight) and German buzz bombs came overhead and I thought, 'if they knocked the top off this building, here I'd be, nude in the tub!' I don't remember many bombings, but then you kind of got used to them too. You'd hear them off in the distance.

"After a while the work became too much for me, and Annabelle Grover came to work with me as a second secretary. Her last name was Grover and she later married Mr. Stover!" A phone interview with Annabel in 2014 clarified that she actually arrived in Bletchley Park on D-Day, June 6th, 1944. She, just like Bev, had been working in the Pentagon and volunteered when the opportunity arose to work in England. She was 25 at that time, a year younger than Bev. Annabel also went to work in London at regular intervals. They were also joined briefly by Dorothy Aldrich, a WAAC in uniform, a bit older than Beverly and Annabel, and not a secretary. Dorothy was also billeted at the White Hart Hotel, and Annabel in a home in Bedford.

Regarding Annabel – as of late 2015 she is still alive and well, living in Alexandria, Virginia, and in touch with Bev, who says, "She and I are the only ones alive, as far as I know, who worked together in Hut 3 at Bletchley. Of course we were younger than the officers, who have all gone ahead." Beverly has also explained that she, Annabel, and Dorothy were the only American women in Bletchley Park as far as they remember.

Regarding Dorothy: "Because she was in uniform she stood out and got more attention than I did, where I'd had it all before. The American army were the 'bee's knees' in England. So I was jealous of her, which is too bad, because she was older and kind of lonely. But I wasn't very happy to see her so I was kind of horrible and unfriendly to her, though I did apologize later". They do seem to have become friends and done many things together later on, as seen in her letters. Dorothy returned to the US after the war, and to her home state of Iowa. She later married, lived in Florida for some years, and died in 1989.

CHAPTER 8

Enjoying England

As well as all the hard work she did at Bletchley Park and in London, Beverly found time for an incredible number of interesting people and activities. Then as now, it seems, life was good and satisfying for her only if the hours were full and the time with friends ample. As well as the Americans Beverly worked with, she got to know many British folk, including her colleagues at Bletchley.

As far as the most famous people of Bletchley, such as Alan Turing, Bev certainly remembers the names – but didn't get to know any of them well, partly because of the solid wall of secrecy that kept them all apart much of the time. She has been fascinated to learn more about some of them later on and is glad that some of these stories are coming out. See Chapter 19 for more on this.

"One British woman who became a very good friend was Pauline Burrough, (met on the ride to work) who later married Hugh Lee, a British Navy officer. He was not at Bletchley, but I met him and he was a very nice guy. She was too, and still is!" Pauline worked in administration in the office at the main building, and also worked on billeting and transport. Later on, Bev spent time with the Burrough family at their home near Chichester, enjoying the countryside and going to a play performed locally.

"Someone I met through Pauline was Barbara Abernethy. I didn't know her terribly well there, but in some ways she was the spirit of Bletchley. She was the personal assistant to the Director, Commander Alistair Denniston. I later learned that she was one of the first to open it up in 1939 and one of the last to leave in 1945. She worked in the main building, in which there was the dining room where we went for meals. We also had plays, dances and concerts – in that same dining hall. There was quite a lot of night life one way and another.

"Angela Stacey and I became good friends. She worked at Bletchley and lived in a very nice house outside of town. Angela's father had died, and she was living at home with her mother. We kept in touch for a while. Once in a while she'd have petrol for her car, and I'd ride with her – very nice instead of in the 'break'.

"One night, I'd gone out to their house for supper on my bicycle. After supper I got on my bicycle to ride back to town, in the blackout of course, and I missed the driveway somehow and landed in the duckpond! (chuckles). They'd been standing in the doorway to see me off and heard the splash and all the noise, and came rushing out and had me come back in and spend the night so I didn't have to ride back in wet clothes.

"I really got teased about this because the word got around town. One day after this incident I asked the lady at the hotel if she had an ironing board and she asked me, 'What do you want to do – put a diving board on the back of your bicycle?'

"I got invited to peoples' homes for meals, very generous of them, given rationing. But sometimes they had shot the meat themselves."

Another friend, Elizabeth Everard, invited Bev to her family home near Coggeshall, in Essex, for the afore-mentioned "first 2 days off" that she had had, in April 1944. The scrapbook description bears repeating in full. "The house is a simply fascinating abbey – built by Cistercian monks in the 12th century – in the real country. Everything about it is charming, and is far beyond my powers of description. I slept in a huge four-poster bed where Elizabeth served me breakfast in bed both mornings (at 11am!). We went for a cook's tour of Coggeshall on our bikes in the pouring rain; met lots of swell people; went to a very 'posh' dance (given by the general of the 9th US bomber command); ate superb meals; picked flowers; collected eggs, and were generally lazy. All very special and ne'er to be forgotten!" Then she refers to traveling back to "the factory". She enjoyed another weekend of relaxation in Coggeshall later that year.

Elizabeth Burbury, who also worked in Hut 3 as a WAAF officer (British Women's Auxiliary Air Force), was a good friend, who later married Capt. Robert Slusser of the US Army in June of 1944, at the Brompton Oratory in London. Bob Slusser had been one of the first officers to work with Taylor and McKee in Hut 3, so Beverly knew him well.

Diana and Bill Marchant (the English deputy chief of Hut 3, and a former master at Harrow School) and their family became good friends. They lived not far away in Bedfordshire, and Bev visited their home on several occasions, including for the christening of their younger son, Timothy, in April, 1945. Telford Taylor and Ted Hilles were also present for this event, as shown in a group photo taken that day.

Beverly (white shirt in front), Diana Marchant and son Charles next to her. Telford is the tallest in the back at left with Bill Marchant next to him, center back. Front row left is Ted Hilles, Telford's deputy.

Peter Calvocoressi was another British colleague in Hut 3 with whom Bev became friends and kept in touch for many years. He came first as deputy head of Hut 3 under Jim Rose, and later became head himself. Peter wrote his recollections of these wartime experiences in *Threading My Way* (1994).

There was a Thanksgiving dinner celebrated in Potterspury, a village about 10 miles from Bletchley, where a group from the park were billeted in an old stone farmhouse, with about thirty Americans taking part. Place cards for each one were drawn by another colleague, Bill Hohenthal, and Bev's card is saved in her scrapbook.

Lang Van Norden also worked at Hut 3. He was from New York, had attended Princeton and studied law at Yale before getting into cryptanalysis as a way of choosing what his military path would be. He and Bev clearly became good friends and enjoyed each other's company – since she describes two different day-long bike trips they did together. Once they went to the Whipsnade Zoo in Bedfordshire, where they "saw all the beasts, and (coming across a fairground), rode all the rides"! Then on a spring day in 1945, Lang and Bev did a 35 mile bike ride through the English countryside – enjoying lambs, views, spring flowers, a pub lunch in one old inn and tea in another – ending up at the Marchants' home for supper. Lang returned to his billet after dinner, but Bev spent the night with the Marchants. They were teased about this later as both had signed the guest book that same evening.

A British military colleague called Colonel Clark was also billeted at the White Hart. He became a good friend of Bev's and decided to write to Harry to tell him how his fiancée was doing. Unfortunately, and most unwisely, he wrote to Harry on the hotel stationery. "That's how Harry found out where I was, which he wasn't supposed to know! And he wrote me a letter to the hotel, and boy, I was mad. I really laid him out in lavender for that! That was a breach of security, and I'm sure the whole war foundered upon that!", she added smiling.

The theater was enjoyed whenever possible, and there are playbills from at least six plays in the scrapbook, and mention of many more, as well as reference made to many films seen. She also took in other sights on her "weekly jaunts into town", which is how her work in London was described to the family. Walking the Embankment and around the City of London, climbing to the very top of St. Paul's Cathedral, visiting Madame Tussauds, seeing Dicken's Old Curiosity Shop, and attending Easter Sunday services at St. Paul's Cathedral on April 1st, 1945, all get mention in her scrapbook. Somewhere along the way Bev also fitted in visits to Oxford and Cambridge, and greatly preferred Cambridge it seems.

Other adventures included going by herself (via bike and train) to visit Sulgrove Manor, George Washington's ancestral home near Oxford; going with friends to visit Leamington Spa and Warwick, where she loved the castle; and another trip with friends to Stratford-upon-Avon where they toured the town, had lunch, and saw "As You Like It" performed. She also visited friends in Lincolnshire at one point and was very impressed by Lincoln Cathedral.

There were also many events at Bletchley Park itself, such as 'Salute the Soldiers Week', concerts, teas, dinner parties, dances, and an unforgettable baseball game between some of the Americans and the Brits at Bletchley. Bev has several photos of the American team at this event, which included many of those she worked with and was friends with. There is also a sheet of instructions written, says Bev, "for the edification (?) of the British" by one of the American team, Al Friendly (later Managing Editor of the *Washington Post*). It is entitled "Baseball: Child's Guide to Customs, Conventions and Polite Usages of the Game." One example of a rule for batters reads: "On making a hit, bat should be dropped, not, repeat not, carried to first base. It is considered rude, however, to purposely hurl the bat at the catcher's head more than twice in one game."!

One anecdote that must be shared – Bev was invited at one point by the Director of Bletchley to go to a costume party for all who worked there, and, in desperation, the only thing she could think of as a costume was to be a devil in her red flannel pajamas, that had feet and a drop seat! She took some red underpants and sewed them into a head cover with pencils stuck in for horns and used an unbent coat hanger covered in red tape as her tail. "It was far and away the most comfortable costume I have ever worn, but it was a little discouraging when people kept saying how 'sweet' I looked. However, I darn near fainted when I was awarded a prize!"

At least twice, once in Jan. 1945 and again on July 4th of that year, Beverly and some friends hosted a party at the White Hart, the latter co-hosted by Annabel and Dorothy, with 80 or 90 guests attending. The guest list survives. That July party was also on the eve of the first British Election Day in 10 years, so it was a festive day for all.

It is no surprise that with all this activity even Beverly's mother, Elsie, expressed concern in a letter about her intense schedule. Bev's response? "Els, for GOODNESS' sake don't be perturbed about my rushing around, knitting, etc. You ought to know by now that I ain't happy unless I have too much to do. Life would be so dull otherwise!" She knew herself well.

An aspect of life in Britain at that time that was very important was food. Like everyone else, Beverly had her ration book and had to produce it for the people at the hotel. There were certainly shortages and restrictions on many things. At one point, soon after receiving a letter from her father describing Thanksgiving, Beverly wrote back with a request "PLEASE DO NOT WRITE TO ME DESCRIBING SUPERIOR CULINARY EFFORTS! Dad's casual description of their 'brunch' on Thanksgiving day was almost too much for me!" So it's clear that she was feeling some deprivation.

There is an amusing exchange in the letters and scrapbook regarding mice and her battle against them. Some packages had come in mid-December '44, and Bev was planning to keep them to open at Christmas. But, "the damn mice are much more impatient for Christmas than I am, and have investigated both of them as they contained food. I stayed up half of the last 3-4 nights chasing the rodents around my room brandishing torches, bicycle pumps, and anything else I could lay my hands on. I already have one tin box for food and have been promised another one, and today I bought a trap." Later there are references to a contest she was having with a friend to see who could catch more mice. She was ahead at that point by nine bodies!

At Bletchley Park they got pretty good food in the dining hall. Still, there was great delight expressed when any edibles came in packages from the US, and since oranges were a rare treat, each one they did get was savored, and the attractive tissue wrappings saved in the scrapbook. Another comment in Bev's words, "Dear Mrs. Firth, the manager of the White Hart, one night produced some corn on the cob, very proudly because she knew Americans liked it. I think it was feed corn because it was so tough, but I was so touched and put on a brave face to eat it."

There was certainly great rejoicing when the Grosvenor House mess hall in London, for a long time open to "officers only", opened in March 1945 for meals to all Americans who worked with the military. It was a mammoth cafeteria with American food, so huge that it was dubbed 'Willow Run' after Ford's production plant in Michigan. Apparently the food was brought in from America, delicious, and cheap – a typical meal costing only about 25 cents.

A final special adventure is the one holiday Beverly had during her time in Britain, just after the war had ended. She and two other women from Bletchley spent nine days in St. Ives, Cornwall, in south-west England, in late summer or early fall of 1945. They seem to have had a marvelous time, "doing nothing but eating, sleeping, sunbathing and hiking", and also managed an overnight trip from there to the Scilly Isles, off the tip of Cornwall – flying the 30 miles there and returning by boat. It would appear that there was a cottage in St. Ives used for military folk to have vacations in, and that is where Bev and friends stayed.

CHAPTER 9

The War Draws to a Close

By April 1945, two themes, one global and one personal, appear in Beverly's letters and records that indicate a page was turning in her life.

First of all, world events were moving to a new phase. President Roosevelt died on April 12th, and of course Beverly, along with all her fellow Americans in England, was deeply saddened by this event. She actually attended the memorial service held in St. Paul's Cathedral on April 17th. After this, other events occurred rapidly – ushering in "the beginning of the end". By late April Mussolini was assassinated, in early May Hitler committed suicide; and then on May 8th, VE Day (Victory in Europe) was celebrated as the war in Europe came to an end.

On the more personal front, Beverly received a letter from the War Department on April 18th amending her travel orders to read that she would be expected to return to Washington by July 19th. Interestingly, she and her friends Pauline and Molly had planned, with the help of Thomas Cook travel agents, a vacation in Scotland together that summer. But, as she puts it, "Pauline transferred to London, Molly learned that she was to be posted to the States, and my orders expired. Ergo – no trip."

In fact – ever since she had arrived in England, Beverly had been planning how to reconnect with Harry and how/where/when they would get married. On January 19th, 1944, just three weeks after her arrival in England, she had opened an account at a London bank with a deposit of £25. The actual deposit slip is pasted into her scrapbook, with a note saying "The start of the 'Get Me to Iraq As Soon As Possible Aprés La Guerre Fund'."

Regarding some dresses that had been sent her, but delayed in uncertain wartime mail, Bev wrote the sender, not to worry if they were delayed because "they'll be nice for Iraq – in fact will be the basis for my trousseau!!!"

At a dinner party Bev attended in the spring of 1945, a friend wrote place cards with a poem for each guest, and Bev's read as follows:

There was a young lad from Iraq
who was bright as a new brass tack.
He woo-ed and won
Our Bevo 'by gum'
Now she's starting to pack for Iraq.

Throughout the almost two years Bev was in England letters had travelled regularly between these two, and also between their families. Bev got cards, photos, and letters from Harry's mother and even from his brother, Dick, who was serving in the Pacific. Harry got letters from Bev's parents and even got into deep philosophical/theological exchanges with his father-in-law-to-be over the morality of the war, where Christians should stand in these matters, and other such weighty topics.

Despite her busy work and social life, and the breezy tone of most of her letters, at least the ones written to the wider family, Bev clearly missed Harry, and home and family, a great deal – from her parents and sisters, aunts and uncles, to the little nephew and niece – Peter and Wendy Prindle, growing up without her seeing them. In a letter to her mother in Jan. 1945, she wrote the following: " . . . I felt the same way about this Christmas as you did! Though nothing could have been grimmer than last year – and nothing (superficially) gayer than this, this year I missed you all much more. As I wrote Harry the other night, absence certainly makes the heart grow fonder – because much as I love you-uns (and him) – the longer I'm away from you, the warmer my feelings and the deeper my love for you becomes. Although I think that picture of you three chickens (seen here) is absolutely swell, I sometimes just can't look at it – it hurts too much."

Three Kitchens, late 1944

In that same letter she goes into some detail as to her possible future plans, clearly and unsurprisingly a recurring theme from all sides. She explains how she and Harry had considered getting married in Lisbon, but felt it was too rushed and too complicated. She says however, that getting married in Basra, Iraq is another story, and not at all impossible. "But don't worry, mommy dear – if nothing else, realizing how close I came to making mistakes before, I promise you that I won't rush into it. The Van Esses (Harry's mentors in Iraq) have invited me to stay with them for several months if I want to, and we really <u>don't</u> expect to tear up the aisle the first week I am there. There again, <u>if nothing else</u> – there will be all sorts of technical complications, and (from what I hear) the climate and general atmosphere of Basra are not conducive to one's thinking that all is rosy and wonderful if it really isn't. I have (although not happily) faced squarely the possibility that in this time apart, living with very different kinds of people and under very dissimilar conditions, we both may have changed – so much that we would realize that it wouldn't work (but I hope not!)."

In another letter (March 3rd, '45) Beverly reflects even more about their relationship and also what it will mean to her to be the wife of a missionary, since she is not at all certain about her faith. "As for Harry and me – one doesn't ordinarily pick one's husband because of his occupation, now does one? I must say that if he were still planning to teach English at Pennsylvania State (for which he was signed up before he decided to go to Divinity School), I wouldn't have any qualms, doubts, or what have you, about us at all. If <u>nothing</u> else did, the facts that (a) I'm reconciled to waiting so long, (b) I'm quite content to lead the kind of life I am leading now – rather than the mad gay one I thought it probably would (and easily <u>could</u>) be, and (c) I've been faithful to him – with two minor exceptions, the second of which was in October (and about both of which he's been awfully nice) – those things would convince me that I love the lad very much." More on those "exceptions" later.

The letter continues, "It wasn't a 'shock' to find that I myself will be classified as a missionary, as I fully realized that. It was just that I've been more or less pulling a 'Scarlett O'Hara' on that chapter of my life, and it was more than a little staggering to think that the time had come to begin to write that chapter – when I didn't even know a 'good opening sentence'. It certainly is a relief to know that I will be able to do some research first – even though what that really means is that I can procrastinate a little longer!" By "pulling a Scarlett O'Hara" one can only presume that Beverly was referring to the line "After all, tomorrow is another day," at the end of the film *Gone With the Wind*.

"Els, you say that God's love cannot be earned or learned, but just accepted – well (no matter what I say next, it isn't really what I mean) – how can one accept something that she doesn't/can't/won't/or whatever it is, believe exists??"

In early April (in an 'all the family' letter) Bev wrote, "I've taken

Harry, being playful
in Iraq, 1945

a new lease on life as Harry has been able to get hold of some British Air Letter forms which come 3 times faster than anything else. Last week I had 5 letters from him, and I hear two more are waiting for me. Golly, to think that it will be only a matter of months until I see him again (instead of years) – or maybe even weeks, if something doesn't happen about my orders!! – it seems almost too good to be true." In fact it <u>was</u> too good to be true, but she didn't give up hope of getting to Harry soon.

The internal struggles with faith and bigger questions continued for some time. In an amazingly honest and open letter to just her parents and Myra, written on May 3ʳᵈ, 1945, Beverly poured out her heart. "Tuesday (May 1ˢᵗ) was one of the strangest and most interesting days I have ever had, and I want to try to somehow tell you about it. I went into town on the morning train, and right after we left, some babe firmly and solemnly declared that she had just heard that the war really WAS over. Even though I didn't honestly believe her, even the possibility that she might be right this time didn't make me feel the least bit elated, but really rather depressed generally – at the thought of the horrible mess of Europe – and the world in general – the Pacific still to cope with, plus the so far discouraging news about the San Francisco Conference." (This is the conference that founded the UN, and which had convened in San Francisco in late April with delegates from fifty countries.)

She continues by saying she had gotten letters that same day from her father, Myra, and Harry. "Harry's letter was more or less the first serious disagreement we have had – i.e. his not agreeing with my decision to stick it out here until the end when I had a chance to leave, telling me why he thought it important to get out there as soon as possible . . . I don't know how to describe to you the terrific mixed emotions I felt – not knowing whether to be glad or sorry about the war situation, and terrific sense of my really deep love for and gratitude for my wonderful family and Harry, plus complete depression at the state of the world – BUT with it all was an overwhelming feeling of hope and optimism for the future. That day for the first time I completely, sincerely and honestly began to want to 'get cracking' on the spiritual side of my life. I didn't actually feel 'like a new woman'. But had a very definite hope and faith that I sho 'nuff can be one (some day).

"As I've told you before, I'm sure, since I've been here I have been saying prayers every night, for the first time in YEARS – but the most regular part of my prayers is not only to ask God to help me believe in Him, but to help me really sincerely WANT to – which probably sounds quite screwy, but that's the way it is. However, Tuesday seems to have cleared up the latter part of that problem, and I now feel sure that the former really will come in time."

Her search for a deeper meaning and purpose for her life continued throughout her later months in England, and at some point in 1945, probably in the autumn, she made a decision to try and put her life in God's hands and seek His wisdom and direction for what she should do. This was a gradual process, and sprang in part from her observations of life at Bletchley Park and in her military community, and partly from what she saw in Germany when she was sent there soon after the war. Of course the fact that she was soon to be married to a minister, and was to be a missionary herself also played into this change of heart. She was supported in this by friends she had made in the MRA group in London, particularly Mary Richmond (later Wilson).

Bev also wrote, in her May 3rd letter, of her discomfort around some relationships she had seen. "One night last summer I was discussing with one of our lads (Hank) how disgruntled I was to see the way the Yanks (particularly the married ones) 'carry on' over here, etc. The boy to whom I was talking is very, very much in love with his wife, and is one of the few people I have seen who is <u>completely</u> faithful to her. I told him that he, and a couple of others, did my soul good – and were more or less my ideals, etc. To which he replied that he thought I would come under the same category. That brought me up with a start, and I broke down and confessed that I had gone off the straight and narrow once a couple of months previously when I had become involved in a necking session. And it had happened one other time too. Neither time, just as if you hadn't guessed it, was I completely sober – but both times I kept thinking about Harry the whole time. However, after talking to Hank, I did write to Harry about it – and it certainly took a big weight off my mind. He (Harry) was, of course, very sweet about it, but even if he hadn't been, nothing he could have said could have made me feel any worse than I did already – I really went through my own private little hell for days after each episode."

It seems that Beverly was beginning to understand the link between the personal and the global, and the difference one's personal life could make to a bigger picture. Although she didn't know it until long after the war, her boss Telford Taylor was having an affair with a young married Englishwoman while in England, as were many others. It is not surprising that as a lively, attractive, fun-loving young woman surrounded by masses of men, many of whom she got to know very well, there might be attractions and temptations in both directions. In a later letter, Bev writes of a young man she knew who thought he was in love with her; and another who actually proposed to her, although he was very aware that she was engaged. It does seem interesting that these issues troubled her largely in a wider framework of the war and the world situation.

In this context, it's worth noting that although Bev actually happened to be in London on VE Day, she was not feeling at all well and had to work until mid-afternoon when, en route to the train back to Bletchley, she had to walk through Piccadilly Circus where "I saw, heard and felt enough celebrating to last me a long time!"

In the post VE Day period things began to change at work as many of those she had known at Bletchley Park earlier were coming back from their various missions to wrap things up. Telford Taylor had gone back to Washington for a time, and Ted Hilles was "holding the fort – his first problem being about 40 jobless bodies on his hands. As you can imagine, things are pretty much in a state of confusion – aside from our office looking like and sounding like the baggage room at Grand Central Station most of the time, people (mostly British ones, that is) are leaving every day, and it's getting harder and harder to find familiar faces." She also wrote,

"One of our lads came back the other day and gave Annabel and me each a very pretty little nut-dish/ashtray effect which he had 'liberated' from the dining room cupboard in the 'Eagles' Nest' (Hitler's mountain retreat). Aside from being attractive, they sho 'nuff have historical and interest value, and will be pretty fancy to hand down to our grandchildren!" Sadly, Bev's dish has gotten lost in various moves, but Annabel still has hers.

Meanwhile, through all of this, the uncertainty of the personal future continued – Bev was still trying to find a job in Iraq that would get her out there, trying to plan a wedding, and to work things out with her family in the US, and Harry in Iraq; all the while with no knowledge of what would be possible and when. While wrestling with all of this, she also got the news that one of the men she had known from the Pentagon had committed suicide. He was "one of the people whom I most admired anywhere . . . and the news has shocked and stunned me an awful lot. It has certainly helped to crystallize my decision about MRA – to try and help make the world a better place where people (especially wonderful people like Johnny) just don't do things like that."

By late June Beverly seemed resigned to the fact that it was highly unlikely she would be able to get to Iraq from England for a variety of reasons. She felt sad, but much worse for Harry, as she at least would be going home to her family. At this point she thought she would return home by July 19th, as per her orders in April.

Then came word that in fact they needed her to go to Frankfurt, Germany for a week or ten days to help Edmund Kellogg finish his work there. Ed had been one of the early Americans into Bletchley, became an advisor to the US Ambassador in Paris, then assistant to the American Ambassador on the Allied Control Council for Berlin. Now he had lots of paperwork to deal with in Frankfurt before he could go to Berlin.

But before Beverly could get her papers and clearance for that task, two other things happened. First Ted Hilles had asked if she would be willing to stay on a few more months in England to wrap things up, rather than having to bring in a new person and train them. Bev, convinced that her orders wouldn't have any chance of being extended again, casually agreed. To everyone's surprise – Ted and Bev are told her orders <u>have</u> been changed and so she would stay based in England at least until October. Here's how she wrote about this change of plans. "Since I couldn't get to Iraq, I thought I might just as well stay here and finish this up as to go and start looking for another job in New York. Of course, Harry's staying out there for the extra year (which he had volunteered to do) puts <u>rather</u> a different light on the matter! When he signed up for it, he didn't realize that I wasn't practically there, and when I signed up to stay here, I didn't know he wouldn't be home by next summer."

The other event was Beverly's 27th birthday on July 8th, celebrations for which seem to have gone on for some time. After enjoying all the cards and gifts that had come from her family, she went to work as usual. "My working day was started off by being roundly kissed by several of the lads, and then a pink carnation corsage from one of them which I wore all day. Then around 3:45 in came Ted (Hilles) with the whole crew behind him singing and bearing a decorated fruit cake, gifts and a card that 'all but' brought tears to *mes yeux*! Printed on it was 'Never has one so small brought so much happiness to so many, in so short a time!' Then, by way of proving what a very well-behaved little girl I yam, a joint effort in the form of a poem.

There was a young lady named Kitchen
Who was winsome and young and bewitchin'
If we weren't so sure
She'd keep constant and pure
We'd all stay around and keep pitchin' !!!"

It is very telling that these men, with whom she had worked all these months, held her in such high regard and affection, and all wanted to let her know that before they scattered at war's end.

CHAPTER 10

Germany

It was July 19th before Bev finally flew off to Frankfurt along with eleven other passengers, of whom she was the only female or civilian. Although the trip was an uncomfortable one as they were in bucket seats amongst boxes of supplies, she was met in style at Frankfurt in a 'very plush diplomatic car' which some of her colleagues there had gotten hold of. Her description continues, "Although we have taken over almost all of the large habitable buildings in the whole city, the center of activity is the Compound, which is <u>completely</u> taken over. The main building is a large and very glam I.G. Farben office building – very similar (and frankly, better looking) to the Pentagon. Behind it are beautifully landscaped buildings with a large lily pond in the middle, and on the other side is the mess – a large, light, airy, extremely pleasant building. It has two large dining rooms, a super snack bar (which is open 22 hours a day and serves real ice cream and <u>iced Cokes</u>!), a bar, and a huge open-air balcony effect. 'Tis there that we eat all our meals."

Finding a place to stay seemed to simply involve searching nearby homes that already had been commandeered by the Americans, locating an empty room, and settling in there. She ends up with a nice room and is later picked up to go for dinner by 'the lads', who are bearing a bouquet of roses that they 'liberated'. Bev adds, "In case you ain't heard, anything to which anyone helps himself is 'liberated'." One can only imagine the feelings of those from whom it was liberated. The whole experience of being in Germany made a deep impression on Bev that lasted for years. Later, she often told her family how she kept wondering, as she lay in her bed, where those people were whose home she was in, and what had happened to them. It felt very strange to be surrounded by their personal belongings left behind, including the hand-made coverlet under which she slept.

Beverly also felt awkward in other ways while in Frankfurt. "To say that I feel like a sore thumb around here definitely goes under The Department of Understatement, as I am the only female (and almost the only person — other than Germans, displaced people, etc.) who wanders around in civvies. Everyone else is in some sort of uniform — which sometimes makes it grim, funny and embarrassing in turn. When I wander around in the streets with any one of the lads, everyone else thinks it's a case of fraternizing and there are usually inappropriate remarks. On the whole, anyone to whom I have spoken has very little good to say for fraternizing. In fact, to be quite realistic about it, as they say 'there can only be one reason for it'. It's really a strange feeling, because cleaning women, workers, etc. are — for the most part either enlightened Germans or P/Ws (Prisoners of War). The waiters and waitresses in the mess are, I believe, entirely D/Ps (Displaced Persons), but you never know whether they are Poles, Russians, French, or something else — so if French fails, I have to resort to sign language. The food in the mess is incredibly good.

"Riding in military vehicles here is not only <u>not</u> verboten, but is the ONLY means of transport, except that, of course, everything in which I ride is stopped to figure out what on earth I am doing there." Much later on, Bev admitted to her family that when she rode in these vehicles there was occasionally a loud 'ping' to be heard. When she asked about it, she was told that sometimes angry Germans had strung piano wire across streets to hit Allied soldiers in the neck as they drove by and decapitate them! So the jeeps and other vehicles had a sharp blade vertically mounted in front to cut the wires as they passed, and that is what she was hearing – very sobering.

"The most 'cheerful' news I've picked up so far is that the Army takes no responsibility whatsoever for anyone who goes outside the Compound in civvies. If one is in uniform, the M.P.s keep an eye on you, but, naturally, can't be expected to otherwise. So if I don't come home you'll know that I've either been picked off by a werewolf or scalped by the Wermacht for fraternizing with the Allies! Just to ease your minds a little bit, though, I haven't (nor won't) go off the premises alone, and usually whoever I'm with has a weapon."

Once again, despite the grim situation they were in, Bev and her friends seem to have had some fun. Apart from anything else, she encountered various people she had worked with at Bletchley Park. One day, for example, "Ed (Kellogg), Pete (Calvocoressi), and I went for a walk in a nearby park which is the grounds of the (now completely gutted) Rothschild residence. We sunbathed on the lawn for a while and finally pulled into the office again – only to find Bill Bundy and two other old friends from England had just blown in from Paris." Another day, a WAF friend managed to "lay on an RAF truck to take Ed, herself, and me over to Bad Homburg to visit another friend based there. There we swam in a perfectly beautiful pool and I christened my lurverly new bathing suit."

Bev, Ed, Ray, and Pete also visited Friedrichshoff Castle in Kronberg which had become the Allied Officers Club. "The grounds are perfectly beautiful – lots of tall trees, mostly pines (which made me homesick for NH) and remarkably well kept up grounds. Ed and I went for a swim before dinner and then joined the others in the dining room, with beautiful linen table cloths, NAPKINS (monogrammed with the family crest), lovely engraved silver, delicious food – loads of butter, real <u>cream</u>, and we were served by very cute little German lasses of about 16, most of whom spoke very good English – all completely pre-war. After dinner we sat out on the terrace watching a full moon come up over the pine trees – the while the little waitresses joined a bunch of the lads with a guitar and sang all the old German songs. The whole thing seemed rather like a dream – to think that less than three months before we had been waging bitter war with those very same people, and then <u>this</u>."

An expedition of a very different sort took place in the city when they "went on a bomb-damage tour of the residential section, which is bad enough, but the main part of the city is practically unbelievable. It is the weirdest feeling to drive past and through block after block of what was once a large city and is now nothing but one huge pile of rubble after another. 'They say' that Frankfurt, although <u>one</u> of the worst, isn't THE worst-hit city, but I really don't see how anything could be much worse. It honestly makes you feel a little ill to think that human beings could survive a thing like that. Where people live now is a great mystery. In the Compound, for instance, the people who lived in the houses and apartments here were given just 4 hours to clear out, but where they went no-one seems to know. Anyone who says that this is going to be a hard winter definitely knows whereof he speaks. For example, we get as much as we want to eat at the mess, whereas the average German ration is between 800 - 1000 calories a day, which is bad enough when supplemented by what fresh fruit and vegetables they can get now. A man who is working on the agriculture side of things told us that literally no canning factories are now operational. Besides which, living in half-standing buildings in this kind of weather is one thing, but in freezing weather, with little or no kind of heat, is something else again. All in all, it is anything but a pleasant picture."

US soldiers in the bombed streets of Frankfurt

Bev adds, "Of course this is a fascinating experience, but it is just such an unnatural existence that I am honestly grateful that I'm not slated to stay here permanently – it's almost a feeling of suspended animation and seems unreal in a terrible sort of way – when you see how very luxuriously and comfortably we are living, and then compare it with the Germans' existence. The countryside is, of course, very very lovely and the now time-worn GI expression to the effect that the Germans have everything, why should they have wanted to try and get more, etc., is very understandable."

As if she hadn't had enough adventures during this trip, Bev left Frankfurt after 12 days and flew to Paris, again in bucket seats, where she was told by the ATC (air transport) officer that she had to wait two days for transport to England. This could have been bad news, but she was presented with a voucher for two nights at a hotel on the Rue de Rivoli right across from the Tuilleries. A pretty amazing, if surreal, wrap-up to her extraordinary experience in Germany. Of course, being Bev, she also connected up with an old friend, Bill Carnahan, who took her to have dinner in the apartment where he and his wife lived on the Ile de St. Louis, "a stone's throw from Notre Dame". The next day she spent sightseeing and also looked up more old friends from Bletchley, now based in Paris, and went with them to see the Eiffel Tower, the Louvre, and other sights.

She was delighted that on the final leg of this trip, back to England on August 2nd, " . . . it was really swish, as we were in a plane with reclining seats – all most comfortable and elegant."

CHAPTER 11

Next Steps

Things were quite different everywhere once the war was fully over. Bev wrote the family on Aug, 16th, heading the letter "V-J plus one" (Victory over Japan Day, and thus the end of the war), and writing, "AT LAST it's all over, and such a wonderful feeling it is to realize that there'll probably never be another war again!"

A letter from Harry to the Kitchens (dated the same day) shares his take on this moment, sadly more realistic in prediction than Bev's. "Well, the fighting has stopped on all fronts, whether peace has come remains to be seen. We have thanked God that the suffering and killing has ceased and yet the potentialities are present for another outbreak unless we do something about it. I do hope Americans will be big enough to exercise real Christian love toward our enemies so that there may be real forgiveness. Otherwise the seeds of resentment and damaged pride will be planted in the hearts of Japan and Germany to appear in another war. It is not easy for a victorious army to forgive, and such hell as has been caused in Japan, but at any cost it is easier than fighting another war."

Bev's letters through September, October, and November indicate that she still seemed to be working hard, and playing hard – with descriptions of meals out, visits with friends, concerts, cricket games, etc – as well as the wedding of her friend Pauline Burrough, and the farewells to many of the folk she had been working with who were heading home. Because of this, in early September they moved the remains of their office crew into a smaller room in Hut 3. One of those who left was Annabel, who was going to Nuremburg to be Telford Taylor's secretary during the war crime trials there. Taylor[4], who was to be one of the prosecutors (and later Chief Prosecutor), had asked one of them to go with him, but Beverly wanted to get home to America, while Annabel was keen to go, and did so happily. It was a sad time in a way as all these folks who had worked so closely were departing in every direction, not knowing if or when they might meet again. "We're still saying goodbye to people right, left and center, and it ain't good at all. I used to joke gayly about being the last body to walk out of these gates, but I don't joke about it any more <u>at all</u>."

One note to add – some five or six years later Beverly received a notice from the War Department instructing her to destroy any lists, addresses, contact information or whatever links she might still have from her days in Bletchley Park. The government was concerned that such information might fall into Communist hands. Despite Harry's protests, Beverly did follow those orders,

---

4 Telford Taylor, who had come to Bletchley as a Lt. Col., was promoted to full Colonel in 1944. He went to Nuremburg as assistant to Chief Counsel Robert Jackson, and when Jackson resigned in 1946, Taylor became Chief Counsel, and was promoted to Brigadier General. The work done by Taylor, Jackson and others created the legal framework for international military tribunals, and for prosecution of crimes against humanity, as encoded in the UN's Nuremburg Principals in 1950.

and regretted it often as it meant she lost touch for many years with most of her friends from that time.

Meanwhile, Bev continued to wrestle with her spiritual life and was trying hard to live differently and seek God's guidance in what she did. She wanted to "go completely all out in it, and not be half-baked" like some she had seen. "I remember I got on my knees (pretty rare for me!) and blurted out something like 'dear God, I want you to run my life'. It wasn't very dramatic, but it was a turning point in my life." This probably took place in Sept. 1945. Later she wrote, "So far, nothing very sensational has occurred, but I guess I'm old enough by now to know better than to expect miracles!" She also seemed to be spending more time with the MRA folks at Hays Mews in London – including meeting several who knew her father from pre-war meetings in the USA.

Beverly adds a memory about visiting Hill Farm in Suffolk, the home of Peter and Doe Howard, Peter being a journalist involved with MRA at that time. "I don't know exactly when it was, but I don't think I would have gone to Hill Farm if I hadn't made that decision. I remember clearly there was a group of people there, and I was sitting on the floor by a big open fireplace. I remember walking through mowed fields with Lucy (later Duncan Corcoran's wife) and talking very openly. She was wonderful, but asked some pretty potent questions. She was a very good friend. Both she and Mary (Richmond, later Wilson) were caring good friends, sincere and wanting to help – but not pushy."

Among the basic principles of MRA was that a person should start the change they want to see in the world in themselves by measuring their lives against four moral standards – honesty, purity, unselfishness, and love. The idea was to clean the slate as much as possible by apologizing or making restitution as needed. Bev told about one experience she remembers very well from that time.

"The first thing I realized about absolute honesty was that because I was under Army orders, though not in uniform, I was able to use the PX, and I bought things. (The PX was the Post Exchange, a shop for the military.) I think I bought a sweater and some stockings, and maybe some cigarettes, and even after I quit smoking I may have bought cigarettes for British people. Well, certainly the clothing I didn't need because I hadn't been there that long, and I gave them to some of my British friends. When I had signed up for whatever I bought I had said it was for my own personal use. So I realized that was not absolute honesty, and I thought if I really wanted to be serious about this, I should go to the PX and tell them. When I got there, the officer in charge was sitting at a desk within a glass cubicle, and all the shopping area beyond. He was sitting in there alone, and I was so ashamed and so embarrassed that I started crying, saying 'I'm so sorry and I'm so ashamed, but I've done this. I can't remember what I bought or how much I spent, but I think I should pay you for it.' He looked very embarrassed and said something like 'I think your conscience has made you pay all you need to pay already.' So I was forgiven my sins. That's the one thing I really remember."

One amusing episode was that Bev had somehow developed an infection on her face, a rather nasty sort of rash requiring that she apply a thick ointment. She wrote her parents that, "So far the only changes apparent because of my trying to 'change my way of living' have been my diseased face! Everyone's telling me that I look sick, tired, or as someone succinctly put it 'like the devil'." She was generally feeling fed-up and frustrated with life – and she was weary, not surprising after her intense schedule for the previous twenty plus months. "I just want to sit quietly with my feet up and RELAX," she wrote home to Myra.

There is also increasing frustration expressed about missing her family, and her fiancé, and having so many misunderstandings and questions in the air between them that she is sure could be sorted out by just sitting down for some long chats. When one thinks about the large number of letters that traveled between them all, despite war, distance, and the two families (Kitchens and Almonds) never having met – it's amazing how much and how well they actually did communicate.

Since Bev was getting ready to head back to the US she was already sending packets of her things home. She had about two months of paid leave owed her on her return, so thought she would spend 2-3 weeks in the East when she returned, and then join her parents and Hopie for a time in Los Angeles where they were based with an MRA group. The plan was that she would then find a job in New York and bide her time until Harry returned.

The final existing letter from England home to the family was written on Nov. 8th, and in it Beverly says she expects to be setting out for home somewhere around the 20th. The exact date of her departure is not known, but she does remember that she was on one of "the big ships, most probably the Queen Mary – which was terrible as we were packed like sardines, with the bunks being triple deckers. We had only two meals a day and those at odd times, as there were so many people on board that was the only way to get them all through the dining rooms. It was NOT the happiest episode of my life!"

Be that as it may, Beverly did get home towards the end of 1945, and although there is no record of what she did in those first months back, she no doubt spent time with her sister Myra (then living with her family in Long Island, NY, as Bill was based in Brooklyn), checked in at the Pentagon to complete her paperwork there; and most probably met Harry's parents in New Jersey.

She then joined her parents and Hope in Los Angeles (LA). During her time there she stayed at the home of George and Polly Eastman, he being a businessman and civic leader in LA who had a large home where several MRA people stayed. Also staying in that home was Ellen Lee Blackwell who became a good friend. In fact, during that time Bev got to know many MRA folk who would become life-long friends, including the Eastmans themselves, whose granddaughter Margaret Smith remains a close family friend.

Beverly also got more and more personally involved with MRA. Although she had written Harry about her decisions of change in her faith life, this was something she felt could potentially cause some problems, as one of the things they had agreed on during their two week courtship was that they really didn't want to have anything to do with the Oxford Group/MRA! Meanwhile, some time after Bev returned to the US, Harry's offer to stay an extra year in Iraq was turned down, so that he could return to the US sooner, complete his final year at New Brunswick Theological Seminary, and then return to the mission field fully ordained.

After some time in Los Angeles, Bev joined a cavalcade of cars that drove together from LA to Mackinac Island, Michigan prior to the summer conference there in 1946. MRA had developed a large conference center on this beautiful island in the Great Lakes starting in July, 1942.

On July 10th, 1946, Beverly and Harry were finally reunited when Harry's ship sailed into New York harbor. There to meet him were Beverly, her mother Elsie, and Harry's parents – Harry and Millard Almond. They celebrated this happy reunion with a special lunch (including for Bev's 28th birthday two days before) at Holland House, a grand old hotel on 5th Avenue in New York City.

CHAPTER 12

A New Beginning – Together

The newly re-united pair understandably felt the need for lots of talking and decision-making about their future. Beverly had already made some decisions about her life and faith, and it seems that Harry had also been doing a lot of similar thinking. In this context, Harry agreed to go with Bev to the MRA summer conference on Mackinac Island.

In Bev's words: "We spent a few days whizzing around seeing various kin and friends and then we were off (driving with Momma Kitch) to Michigan – stopping en route (by way of doing things a bit backwards) at Niagara Falls." Bev calls this 'a bit backwards' because Niagara Falls was a traditional honeymoon destination.

An excerpt from Harry's book will tell the story of what happened next. "It was there, on beautiful Mackinac Island, that I gave my life to God in a fuller way than I had ever done before, making a commitment very similar to Bev's. Admitting that I had not always done a very good job so far, I asked Him to take over.

"Bev and I were faced with a very hard question to consider. We were very different people than we had been on that ship in 1943 when we got engaged. We had both been through deep experiences during the war, and now each had come to a new place of commitment to God. Was our engagement and the love we felt really part of the next step of our lives, or was it just a carry-over from an intense wartime romance? Was it solidly enough based to see us through a lifetime together? Wanting to be sure of this, we painfully put our engagement on hold and really prayed for a sense of certainty as we sought God's leading in this crucial matter." Beverly discovered later that Harry's doubts had been much greater than she realized, and that he came very close to leaving the island, and her, at one point!

But all ended well, as Harry wrote, "After some days of soul-searching and conversations with caring friends, we met with these friends for tea, and in quiet together found the sense of certainty we had prayed for."

Bev's take on all this, as recounted in a widely sent-out letter she wrote a couple of months later entitled The Almond Nuptials, is typically delightfully breezy and original. "We spent four wonderful weeks at the Moral Re-Armament Training Center at Mackinac Island, during which time we became re-acquainted and really faced squarely together the things that go into a marriage that – like the fairy tales say – is happy <u>ever</u> after! We found there were lots of things about ourselves that we either hadn't wanted to tell each other – or that we thought too unimportant. It gave us a brand-new lease on life to get absolutely and completely 'au courant' with each other – even on the most trivial matters (and we're gonna do our durnedest to keep it thataway). Then, and not until then, did we begin to get clear and definite plans for our wedding.

"About August 10th everyone seemed to agree that August 31st should be W-Day. Whew – three weeks and not one preparation made – no invitations, no trousseau, no plans, no nothing! We skeedaddled back to Harry's home in New Jersey (driving all through one night) where we HQ'd for a few days while invitation envelopes were speedily addressed (Harry's whole family and Momma Kitch did most of that noble effort), trousseau rounded up, and more and more plans hatched.

"We finally arrived in Gilmanton (the beloved family place in New Hampshire) exactly two weeks ahead of time – and then the miracles began to pop! Everyone in the town pitched in and offered to help – sewing, cooking, putting up wedding guests, supplying flowers, decorating the church – one seemingly insurmountable barrier after another just quietly dissolved almost magically.

"And here we devote a special paragraph to Momma Kitch and Myra and Bill Prindle. All three of them worked like slaves night and day in preparation – and there was no let-up for them for at least two weeks afterwards. Nothing seemed to be too much for them, and they certainly ought to have special medals for ultra-meritorious service.

"As Poppa and Hopie Kitch were both in Switzerland – where (through the MRA program) they are devoting all their time to helping bring to Europe the new spirit of the things that will make a lasting peace – Bus Reed (that swell uncle of Bev's) gave her away. (A high point of the day for us was talking to the Swiss members of the family on the phone during the reception!!) Myra Prindle was matron of honor and the bridesmaids were Bus's daughter – Mary Caroline, and Ellen Lee Blackwell – a southern belle from Richmond (whom Bev had met in LA). Harry's brother Dick was best man, and ushers were Bob Campbell (a cousin of Harry's), Kelsey Dodd (an old pal), and Bill Prindle. Two days before the wedding we discovered that two young ladies of six, who were very, very excited at the idea of going to a wedding, had for 10 days been practicing marching like flower girls up and down the driveway, so we quickly asked them to do it officially, and they were cute as buttons.

"Bev was planning to wear her Grandmother Kitchen's wedding gown. But one of the big difficulties was what the bridesmaids could possibly get to wear at such short notice. Several sets of bridesmaid's dresses were proffered by friends, but none of them seemed to be just right. To be brief (!), beginning by a remark that Ma K. made more or less in jest, the three girls finally wore costumes of the same period as the wedding gown (found in various attics in Gilmanton), and they looked simply darling.

"Pete Prindle (aged 4, and Bev's godson), in discussing possible wardrobe for the wedding, made the rather shattering remark that he thought he'd probably wear his birthday suit! Immediate further questioning revealed that he referred to a <u>tweed</u> suit that he'd been given for his birthday.

"Another problem was the organist. We had a half-hearted promise from a friend who claimed she really couldn't play and didn't want to – and would only do it in a pinch if we couldn't possibly find anyone else. We weren't very happy about that, but could see no alternative – until 2 days before the wedding, when we discovered that there was a professional organist staying in the next house with friends!! And he most kindly took a 'postman's holiday' and did the honors beautifully.

"An old friend of Harry's, Coert Rylaarsdam, had promised to perform the ceremony – notwithstanding the facts that his wife was expecting a baby the week before <u>and</u> that he was scheduled to speak in Chicago at noon the day before!! Well Coert Jr. (the baby) obligingly arrived on the 22nd, BUT his father could get no plane reservations. However the RR's (railroads) came through and he hit Gil just <u>60 minutes</u> before H-Hour." It is not clear what was meant by H-hour, perhaps 'hitching', but certainly refers to the time of the wedding.

"Even though it was on such short notice (besides being on Labor Day weekend) a large number of our family and friends managed to get there – and it was such fun to see them all, particularly as there were a great many whom we hadn't seen since before we went overseas." Wonderfully, a colleague of Bev's from Bletchley, Bob Slusser, and his English wife Elizabeth, were amongst those attending the wedding.

The happy pair on their wedding day,

The bridal party – from left: Ellen Lee Blackwell,
cousin Mary Caroline Hopkins, Bev and Harry, and
sister Myra Prindle with her daughter Wendy.

The happy pair then honeymooned at Minnewaska, a resort
in the Shawngunk mountains north of New York City near the
Hudson River where Harry had worked one summer. One story
from that honeymoon is that Harry ordered steak and apple pie
for breakfast their first morning there, leaving his bride to wonder
if she would be expected to produce the same each morning in
future!

They then settled down in New Brunswick, NJ in the fall of
1946 for Harry to complete his theological studies. Beverly got
a position as secretary to the President of the seminary, Dr. John
Beardslee. It must have been wonderful for them to have that year,
peacefully in the USA, near family and in an on-campus apartment, to start their life together.

Of course Beverly, always looking to keep things lively, and not liking the drab green of the hallway of the seminary building where they lived, decided to paint the door of their apartment bright red herself. Harry was a bit nervous about the reaction to this when they invited Dr. and Mrs. Beardslee for dinner one night. In fact, when he saw it Dr. Beardslee paused and said "I like that door. Red is my favorite color!"

There is only one letter saved from that seminary year, written Nov. 1946, and it is full of fun, humor, and busy activities as usual. Harry and Bev did seem to be fairly involved with MRA folk, attending meetings, having people to stay, etc. – as well as with setting up their home, enjoying wedding photos sent them, and so on. Harry was doing some preaching at churches in the area, and Bev reports proudly on how well he did.

On May 22nd, 1947, Harry graduated, and was then ordained as a Minister and Missionary on June 1st at Christ Reformed Church in Tappan, NY. They then spent that summer with MRA, first supporting a group with the musical revue *Ideas Have Legs* in Detroit, and then at the summer conferences on Mackinac Island, where the revue *The Good Road* was produced. That fall it was time to prepare for departure to Iraq as missionaries.

More adventures were about to begin, especially as Harry and Beverly were now expecting their first child, due in January, 1948. They originally planned to go by ship and take their household goods, but ship captains seemed leery of carrying a pregnant woman, so they had to fly. They left New York on October 24th, 1947 on an Air France flight, but a booking error resulted in their having to wait in France a week, as 'guests' of the airline, which turned out to be most fortuitous. Amazingly, Vic Kitchen and Hopie were in France with an MRA group, so Harry was finally able to meet his father-in-law and Bev's younger sister. In fact, the four of them together were also able to take part in the first post-war MRA conference in France, which took place in the town of Le Touquet on the English Channel. Quoting again from Harry's book, "The beach was littered with barbed wire and dotted with concrete gun emplacements, grim reminders of the very recent past. Here we met for the first time many who would become friends and colleagues for life." After this unexpected gift of time in France, the couple flew on via an overnight stop in Brindisi, Italy and another in Beirut, Lebanon, finally landing in Baghdad on Nov. 4th. Quoting from a Christmas letter to family and friends written by Beverly a few weeks later, "We pushed on that night by train to Basra, where we arrived the next morning and were welcomed at the station by a large gang from the school who literally swarmed all over the train.

"Although it's cold enough for the fireplace to feel very welcome in the evenings now, this is being typed outdoors in the sun, and it is indeed a unique experience to be here among people whose dress, customs, and language are much like those of Palestine 1900 years ago." This seems a wonderfully appreciative attitude with which to celebrate the lead-up to Christmas and the start of the next stage of their lives.

CHAPTER 13

Basra, Bahrain and Babies

B efore embarking on the narrative of this new chapter, it might be useful to give a little context for events in the tumultuous Middle East into which the Almonds had just arrived. Not only was there anger and anti-western sentiment in Iraq following the former British mandate, and later invasion by British troops in 1941 to protect it against German take-over; but there was also anger at the Iraqi government by its own people over low wages, food shortages, and hardship of many kinds. In January 1948, just months after the Almonds arrived, 300-400 people were killed by the police in the streets of Iraqi cities where they were demonstrating against a recently signed treaty with Britain. Then, when the partition of Palestine and the formation of the state of Israel by the United Nations occurred in May of 1948, many Arab nations, including Iraq, sent troops in opposition to this, leading to further unrest.

Against that background, once again intrepid Beverly was making a start in a totally new part of the world, expecting her first child far from home and family, <u>and</u> needing to learn Arabic as fast as possible in order to take up her task as an effective missionary!

Nevertheless, when asked many decades later about the challenges she faced, she said, "No, I don't remember any very hard things. I know I had a lot to learn – customs, and the language – that was very tough. I remember when I was in England, I had gotten some kind of a book about learning Arabic, and I remember reading 'make a noise like a camel thirsting for water' to get the right sound. I had NO idea." Whether this happy view is due to the dulling of recollection of some hardships over time, or is in fact what she felt then, the memories that endure today are generally wonderful ones.

It is interesting therefore, to read an article written by Beverly for the Arabian Mission magazine about a year after her arrival. Bev was uncomfortable when she re-read it after all these years, feeling her perspective then was somewhat patronizing and judgmental, and she was not sure she wanted it included in this book. Given that it does show her thoughts then as a missionary, and also shows how greatly both her understanding and the world have changed since, she agreed to include parts of it.

The piece is entitled *Arabian Kaleidoscope*. "Do you remember looking into a kaleidoscope when you were a child? Each time you blinked the entire scene had changed to another combination of garish colors and patterns. That is what I think of when I try to record my first impressions of Arabia, and those include sounds and smells as well as scenes.

"Most unkaleidoscopic, however, is the frequency with which the scene is punctuated with spots of black, each spot representing a woman draped in her black abba. Only the very wealthy women have more than one abba and they are made of various materials, some of very fine silk. However, the very poorest (and that means most women in the country) own only one, of heavy, coarse wool, which they wear all year. I remember the strange sensation that came over me during our stop-over in Beirut when I had my first glimpse of little groups of these black-draped figures huddled in the dust, just sitting or squatting listlessly. Waiting? Perhaps, but for what? It gave me a rather depressed, hollow feeling plus more than a little curiosity to know how they themselves feel about their inferior position in this system of society. Under the drab exteriors, however, there are always very bright, usually flowered or figured dresses. And one of the most fashionable practices is to dip hands and feet, as well as hair, into henna dye.

"To make a very brief summary of how they do feel, however, I should say that the huge majority of uneducated people accepts everything as being Allah's will and does not question or aspire to anything higher. The women of the small educated group are beginning to get a little restless and to wish for the freedom and the fun that we westerners have. Very gradually, some of the old customs are beginning to change or disappear as they learn more and more of our ways from movies, magazines and personal contacts.

"Everywhere one sees a great deal of bright blue – the benches in the coffee shops, decorations on the mosques, bits of blue pinned to the clothing or tied to the beds of babies – because blue is a lucky color and keeps off the Evil Eye.

"What struck me next was the amazing cacophony of sound in all these cities. Everyone who drives a car uses one hand for all operations necessary to that art, and the other for tooting the horn constantly. Bicycle bells, too, play no small part in this chorus, as every single bike has a bell or squeeze horn which its owner loves to demonstrate, also constantly." Beverly then describes the loud radios blaring Arab music or news from the many coffee shops, the voices of the street vendors advertising their wares, the shouts of bus and taxi drivers, and " . . . last but not least, there are the scores of little donkeys. They are the chief beasts of burden and their braying and the tinkling of their little bells as they trot along are also familiar sounds.

"So many things are difficult to understand, and during the course of a day one's emotions go from annoyance, to pity, to disgust, to amusement and back again many times. When I say difficult to understand, I mean for us foreigners of course. The Moslem simply accepts everything as coming direct from Allah.

"Like everyone else who has spent any time out here, I have been very much impressed by the generosity and warm hospitality of everyone. It is unthinkable to pay even the briefest visit to the most dilapidated mud hut without having tea, coffee, or sweets of some kind offered to you."

Beverly concluded, "I feel sure that I shall continue to have 'first impressions' for a very long time as there seems to be a never-ending chain of people, places and traditions to be investigated. Certainly the greatest lack in every corner is Christian discipline and love, and it is my daily prayer that there can be more than enough in my life for myself and everyone I meet."

In order to provide a fuller setting for Beverly's other recollections of arriving in Basra, here are some descriptions of the city from Chapter 3 of Harry's book, *An American in the Middle East*. "Basra, Iraq's second largest city and its major port, lies on the west bank of the Shatt al-Arab (river of the Arabs) which is formed when the Tigris and Euphrates merge into one river about 40 miles upstream. Basrah is about 60 miles up from the delta of the river on the Persian Gulf. Basra had three distinct sections at that time, Margil, Ashar (where the mission compound was), and the old city of Basra, that we called Basra City.

"The School of High Hope, the Basra boys' school where I was to teach, was in a compound of about five acres on the north bank of Ashar Creek nearly a mile in from the river. Our garden boasted over 80 date-bearing palms which, in addition to producing delicious dates, provided a partial sun screen for the vegetables and flowers grown by Abu Ali, the gardener.

"Some have called Basra 'the Venice of the East' because of the network of irrigation canals and creeks. These waterways also provided passage for local transport called 'belams', narrow, heavy wooded craft propelled by paddle and pole. We often enjoyed 'belam teas' along the date garden creeks or on the banks of the Shatt al-Arab itself, loading rugs, primus stove, kettle and food aboard for the outing.

Ashar Creek, near the mission compound

"As well as the gardens, the two school buildings, a small building for an alumni coffee shop and gathering place, a playing field, tennis court, servants quarters and the old stone church building, the compound included two houses; the Van Ess and Gosselink homes." When Harry had been in Basra before as a single man, he had rooms in the dormitory with the boys, and had to keep an eye on them; and he had eaten most of his meals with the Van Esses. But of course things were different now.

Returning to Bev's narrative, on arrival in Basra, "We were taken to the mission compound, and to the home of George and Christine Gosselink, where we were to live. The Gosselinks were the second couple in the mission there, and he was head of the school, which Harry would be taking over eventually. Their kids (two sons who were boarders at Kodaikanal School in India, and a daughter at college in the States), would come home for vacations which was fun. There we had a big room with our own bathroom, and a screened porch at the back. The front looked over the street and the creek. On our first or second day there, Harry said, 'Come, I want to show you something.' So we looked out and there was a man walking along, and behind him, his wife – carrying a huge package on her head. Harry said, 'This is the way they do things around here.'

"We had all our meals with George and Chris. They just took us in so warmly and were so good. They were older than us. George and Harry worked at the school, and Chris and I worked with the ladies, including running a club for under-privileged girls from nearby villages. Meanwhile Harry was teaching English and directing the sports program at the school, while also preparing for the mission's second year Arabic exam. We were in one part of Basra, and there was another part of town where the girl's school of the mission was. We had good communication with the people there; Miss Kellian was the head, and another woman, Ruth Jackson, taught there as well.

"I was doing Arabic lessons with Dr. Stanley Milray, a missionary medical doctor, who was mostly retired by then. His wife had died years before, so he lived with the Van Esses in the other house. But he was a dear soul and he was very patient with me. Once when we were struggling over some text, he said, 'My dear girl, don't you know that story?' – some very well known Bible story. He had had some touch with MRA through his brother in England so it wasn't totally unknown to him."

One thing Bev did not have to worry about was any cooking or cleaning, as there were servants who took care of that. "There was a cook, an older man, rather set in his ways. Then Yasser, a younger man, did the cleaning and waiting on table and that sort of thing. They were both very nice and friendly. The older man was a bit gruff, but Yasser was great fun, and very amused at some of my Arabic."

As for adaptations to new foods, Beverly felt it wasn't that big an issue. "One morning at breakfast we found insects in the cereal, and we just took them out and put them aside – not a fuss made! We had a mixture of American and Iraqi food – that's what the Gosselinks did. No problems there. We always had dibbis (date syrup) on the table, made from our own date trees in the compound."

In the final months of her pregnancy, Beverly was getting regular medical check-ups, and this is what she says about the doctors who cared for her. "What I remember was the doctor was a Scottish man at the Maude Hospital. He was the obstetrician I went to, but there was another couple who were both doctors too, the Attishas. He was an Iraqi who had gone to Scotland, where he met a British woman doctor, whom he married. The Scottish doctor was on the hospital staff and so delivered the baby, but Dr. Vic Attisha (Mrs.) was my doctor later. People in Basra were thrilled that there was a woman doctor who could look after the women. Dr. Attisha would learn from her husband at breakfast how to ask the questions she wanted to ask her patients each day, so that was how she learned Arabic. She also learned much local traditional medicine from village women that proved to be very helpful in some cases – and was scientifically proven later.

"Three months sped by, and then Anne was born, at the Maude Hospital in Basra City, on January 28th, 1948. I guess I was having pains so Harry took me in, but the baby didn't arrive until the next day, so I spent one night there in hospital before she came. I remember Harry telling me that he had gone through crowds of protesting students, some of them from his own school, to come see us in hospital. I guess I was there a few days, and then came back home. That's when Haila came into the picture as Anne's Iraqi nanny. She was not trained, but very nice, and a bit older than me. She did not speak any English, but she was patient, and Chris Gosselink was also around to help, and she was fluent in Arabic.

Haila lived in the servant's quarters in the compound, so was nearby when needed.

"Anne was born with a caul over her head. I don't remember if I even saw it. I was certainly told about it, but think they took it off right away quickly. It didn't cause a problem, but it was a surprise. I think people felt it was good luck." A caul is a membrane that remains over part of a baby when it is born, usually over the face or head. It is quite rare, occurring in only 1 out of every 80,000 births, but is generally removed quickly and easily at birth. Many cultures have the belief that cauls bring good luck or are protective of the child, and that was the belief in Iraq. Little Anne was christened and named Beverly Anne after her mother. She was also given the Arabic name *Bushra*, which means 'good news'.

"When Anne was a baby, her father and I would take turns pacifying her when she cried, especially at night. One night we couldn't get her to stop crying, and we had her in bed between us, and both of us were trying to grab her and take her to console her, then we suddenly realized we were pulling the baby in opposite directions! A rather horrible moment. On the whole, Anne was a pretty easy baby. I did breastfeed her, but I didn't have enough milk, so I had to supplement. Dr. Attisha said to me one time, 'If you want to feed that baby on your own, you need to live like a cabbage, and that's not your nature!' She was very nice, and helpful.

"I spent a lot of time working hard on Arabic, while Anne, spending so much time with Haila, began to learn Arabic quickly. I'd sit on the balcony to study and Anne would be playing around me on the floor. One day she grabbed an upright bar on the balcony and it broke and she fell all the way down to ground level. I have never moved so fast in my life as to dash downstairs and get that child. There she was, probably crying, but apparently not hurt in any way. Dr. Milray came right over and examined her thoroughly, but could find nothing wrong. He thought it was miraculous, and all the local people said 'she was upheld by the wings of an angel', and they fully believed that, and I did too. How else to explain it? This was one floor up, with high ceilings, so probably 10-12 feet at least, onto brick pavement. That was amazing."

Writing their annual Christmas letter looking back at 1948, Beverly covers all aspects of life from the proud reporting on the progress of baby Anne, to social life, to politics: "The first part of the year was enlivened by a series of Communist-inspired strikes and demonstrations in which everyone from schoolboys to street sweepers took part. However, military law, following the entrance of Arab forces into Palestine, forced all such feeling underground or to prison. When it will next erupt no one knows."

On a different note, Bev added, "During the summer we continued our language study and usually managed to keep warm enough with the 110-120 F shade temperatures!"

Apart from Harry's work at the school, language study, and the daily routines of life, photos and conversations indicate the Almonds also enjoyed a lively wider social life. Among their mission colleagues, which included those based in Kuwait, Bahrain and Marmara, Iraq, they had many dear friends who remained such for years. Jay Kapenga, for example, had been a seminary classmate and good friend of Harry's and then worked with him in Basra, along with his wife Midge. They also had friends in the British community there, and photos of the Almonds in evening dress at the St. George's Day ball at the British Council, and at an RAF dance, attest to this. The Fletchers (Harry and Doreen) and Campbells (Noel, Dora and their baby daughter Trudi) were British Council folk who also became long-time friends.

Life continued in this manner in Basra for the little family for some time, but with one significant sad loss. When Harry had returned to Basra with his bride in late 1947, he realized that Dr. Van Ess was in very poor health, and in fact this extraordinary man, mentor and good friend died in early summer 1949. John Van Ess had been a towering figure in the mission and in the Middle East since 1902, was the founder of the school, a scholar fluent in six languages, and a teacher and mentor to many, so his death was a terrible blow to the whole community. Soon after, his widow Dorothy left to return to the States, and the Almonds moved into the Van Ess house across the compound. "We just had two bedrooms there – Anne was in one and we were in the other." Bev was now mistress of this household with three servants to manage. There was of course Haila the nanny, Ghulam the cook, and Mustafa the houseboy, in his late teens and passionately devoted to his bicycle! The gardener, Abu Ali, took care of the whole compound and was thus shared with the Gosselinks.

One amusing incident at that time was when a feral cat came into the kitchen and made off with a roast. This was not popular with the cook – so Harry came up with a solution, which he describes in his book. "I rigged up a box held up by a stick with a long string attached, bait was nailed inside the box, and when the cat entered the string was jerked, pulling away the stick. Ghulam remained aloof, as befitted his cook's dignity, until I actually trapped a cat, put it in an old sack and made suitable disposition. From then on Ghulam was an enthusiast. He would sit on the back step, string in hand, with all the devotion of a committed angler, and soon the cats stopped visiting. But we never persuaded Ghulam to close the new screen door he had requested."

The Almonds in the garden in Basra

In the spring of 1950, although Harry was slated to take over as principal of the school in Basra before too long, the Almonds were asked to help out by going to Bahrain to cover for their mission colleagues there, Rev. Edwin and Ruth Luidens, so they could take their allotted year-long sabbatical in the USA. Once the school year in Basra was over in early June, the Almond family, plus Mustafa the house boy and his beloved bicycle, went to Bahrain – across the Persian Gulf, on the ship *Dwarka*. Yet more changes!

Bev's memories of Bahrain are as follows: "We were staying in a big building that was owned by the mission with several apartments in it, side by side, with a long common veranda along the ground floor. There was some open space in front, another building on the left, and our kitchen was in a separate building just behind us. It turned out to be a filthy place – as we found out when the cook died!

"There was also an orphanage that I was responsible for in a building out back, with about 8-10 orphans and an older Bahraini lady who ran it. I was fully in charge of it at one point, for maybe a week or so when she was away. I didn't sleep there then, but I had all my meals there with them during that time. Some of them were teenagers, and some were quite small. I think they must have gone to the local school. I always struggled with my Arabic, but I was able to chat with these children and get along.

"Harry was the pastor of the Arabic language mission church there in Manama, the capital city of Bahrain, and there was the mission hospital, and possibly a school to look after. He also took English language services at the oil company place out of town."

Their house-boy Mustafa did not last long in Bahrain as he got terribly homesick, and that overrode his devotion to the Almond family, so he returned to Iraq, bicycle and all.

While the family were there, Bev became pregnant with their second child, and this is how she recalls the arrival, which occurred on June 6th, 1951. "One morning I took several of the orphans to the souk (market) to buy shoes, and then around lunch time I began to think something was going on. So I went to the Nykerks' house, because they had an air-conditioned room, and Dr. Gerry Nykerk was the mission doctor there and a good friend, along with his wife Rose. I sat in that room, reading or resting, and one of the nurses was keeping an eye on me. Then I went over to the hospital, and Cornelia Dahlenburg, the nurse and a wonderful woman, delivered the baby because the doctor wasn't available." The baby was named Elizabeth Jane, and is usually called Betsy by family and good friends. She was also given the Arabic name *Dana*, the name of a special kind of local pearl, described as "the most perfectly-sized, valuable and beautiful pearl".

Proud big sister Anne
with baby Betsy

"I had a private room with a private toilet, but in order to use the toilet I had to walk over cockroaches on the floor! And people kept coming into the room to see a white baby – it was like a public thoroughfare! It was quite an easy birth as I remember it, much faster than Anne's birth."

While in Bahrain, Bev did continue studying Arabic, but it was a more informal study, and she got much of her practice in conversation with the people she met. One person the Almonds met there was a young man named Mohammed who was interested in learning more about Christianity. There was another American missionary couple also living at the mission building, recent arrivals who were due to go and work elsewhere but got stuck in Bahrain waiting for their paperwork. They were very keen to convert Mohammed and get him baptized, while Harry and Bev cautioned them about pushing too hard or quickly, knowing the rejection and shunning that could follow from Mohammed's family if he did convert. The Almonds simply tried to befriend the young man and shared their own faith and struggles with him, without making demands. The other couple got very angry and publicly said judgmental and condemnatory things about Harry. This left a bad atmosphere, and other colleagues were caught in the middle.

So it may have been with some relief that the Almond family left Bahrain in the summer of 1951, and headed for a break in the mountains of Switzerland.

CHAPTER 14

Caux, Switzerland

Part of the arrangement for Reformed Church of America (RCA) mission families in the Gulf was that they should take a break each year in a cooler climate for their health. Many went to the relatively nearby mountains of Lebanon, but the Almonds chose to take their breaks in Switzerland, going to the MRA conference center in Caux-sur-Montreux, 2,000 feet above Lake Geneva. These were important times of connection for them with friends and even sometimes with family.

They had first gone to Switzerland in mid-August of 1948. That had been seven month old Anne's first flight, and Harry said in a letter at the time, that she appeared to enjoy flying immensely. "We stuffed her in the overhead baggage rack for naps, and in between she bounced around among the passengers."

A letter from Beverly recounts that they flew to Geneva, where they were met by her parents and together took the lovely five-hour boat trip to Montreux at the other end of Lake Geneva. From Montreux they took the steep cog railway straight up to Caux-sur-Montreux and the Third World Assembly for Moral Re-Armament. This former hotel building is in a spectacular setting, with the lake far below, the French Alps across the lake, and mountains all around. Bev wrote, "It would take volumes to describe all that we saw and heard there but, briefly, there were about 5,000 delegates from almost every nation, including Germany and Japan. They had gathered to learn how we can help bring democracy's ideology to the world."

Besides reconnecting with family and friends, some of whom they had met in 1946 at the conference center at Mackinac Island, Michigan, and others from the 1947 stopover at Le Touquet in France, the Almonds made many new friends on these summer visits to Caux.

One of these was a young German woman called Irmgard Fetzer who was secretary to Pastor Hans Stroh, the Protestant Chaplain at Tubingen University. Pastor Stroh had known the Oxford Group before the war and was known to be a man of integrity, so he and others from his church were among the first Germans to be cleared by the Allied occupying forces to leave the country and come to Caux as early as 1946. Irmgard's fiancé had been drafted early in the war and sent to the Russian front where he was killed. It was a very special experience for these two women to meet at that time, just three years after the end of the war, and following Bev's immediate postwar visit to Germany which had made such a deep impression. Thus, when little Anne was baptized that summer by an American friend, Rev. Skiff Wishard, at the small but lovely Protestant chapel in the village of Caux, her godparents were Irmgard Fetzer and Van Wishard (Skiff's son). The friendship with Irmgard continued until her death in the mid 2000s, with Anne and Irmgard reuniting in Caux in 1985 and 2002, and also in England in 1992.

Serendipitously, also present at Caux in that summer of 1948 was Bev's sister Hope, who like their parents was working with MRA in Europe. A wonderful family picture of them all together was taken on the lawn at Caux.

The family together at Caux – Vic, Elsie, Bev
with Anne, Harry, and Hope in front

In 1949 the family again spent time in Europe, one month at Caux, and one month when Harry and Bev went to the Netherlands, while little Anne was left in Caux, being cared for by a Danish friend. They did not go to Europe in 1950, as they had just moved to Bahrain.

Thus, in the summer of 1951, not long after Betsy's birth, and following the difficulties in Bahrain around the issues of Mohammed's conversion, the family again came to Caux. Having completed their time in Bahrain, they planned to return to Basra after the summer and continue with the school and work there.

Betsy was christened at Caux that summer by the Rev. Frank Buchman, the founder of MRA. There were four babies christened together at the ceremony, in the lovely bay window of the great hall at Mountain House. In the international spirit of the place, her two godparents were Brenda McMullen, an American, and Deva Surya Sena, a Sri Lankan traditional musician, both good friends of Harry and Bev's.

Anne joined other pre-school children at the nursery program provided at the center. At some point that summer she told her parents that God had told her that she shouldn't stay at the nursery school with the other children at nap time. At first they dismissed this as a childish whim, but she had such a clear sense of certainty that they decided to respect her decision. Around that time, Beverly also noticed when she checked on the children at night, that Anne was extremely sweaty and feverish. So they talked to Dr. Dick van Tetterode, a Dutch medical doctor friend who was at Caux, and he suggested that they consult a Swiss doctor, Dr. Steiner, a pulmonary specialist, and get her a chest x-ray. This was done, and it was found that Anne had early stage tuberculosis (TB), with a primary lesion in one lung. In fact, fever and night sweats are symptoms of TB, along with coughing and appetite loss. As one might imagine, this was a terrible shock for Beverly and Harry. They concluded that Anne had gotten this disease from her nanny in Bahrain, and later learned that the woman had indeed died from TB.

Dr. Steiner told the Almonds that the best cure for TB was to have complete bed rest, healthy food, and clean mountain air. This was the standard practice for the time. So, after many prayers and quiet times of reflection with friends – Harry and Bev decided to place Anne in a sanatorium called 'Les Melezes' in the village of Leysin – about an hour's drive from Caux up the Rhone Valley. This was a heart-wrenching parting for Harry and Bev, and probably for Anne too at the time, but she has no recollection of it at all. Bev says, "There were tears all the way around!" This family photo was taken as Anne was about to leave for the clinic.

The Almond family in 1951

Anne was to spend the next nine months in Leysin, from the fall of 1951 until the following summer, while the family based in Caux. Her parents were encouraged not to visit her for a while, as she needed to settle, and then after that not too often – as saying goodbye each time was very hard. However, Bev did make regular visits there during those months.

One interesting aspect of this experience was that Anne at that time spoke both Arabic and English (as fluently as any 3½ year old would) – but the sanatorium was in French-speaking Switzerland, and was run by a Russian couple; so she forgot all her English and Arabic during her stay there, and emerged speaking Swiss French with a Russian accent!

All this meant a complete change of plan for the family, as they were due to return to Basra after the summer, and Harry was to take over at the school. Remembering all that they wrestled with at the time, Beverly said, "Well, we'd already been having more and more questions in our own minds about whether being in the mission was where God wanted us to be. The world was in such a mess, and here we were – Americans trying to tell people in the Middle East how to live. People there did say to us, 'Why don't you go home and try to fix things up in America?'. But it was a terribly hard decision as we had such good friends personally in the mission. Then the doctor said that Anne shouldn't go back to that trying climate for at least two years. So that was one thing that helped us think – well, if we aren't going back for two years, should we ever go back?"

As Bev and Harry pondered these questions, and sought clarity in prayer and reflection, they were glad to have friends there in Caux with whom they could talk it all over. The new ways of building bridges and working in equal partnership with those of different faiths that they were seeing demonstrated at Caux were a contrast to the mission mandate to convert others. They felt that this new kind of cooperative work was how they were called to live out their faith in the future. Therefore, they decided to resign from the mission work and to give all their time to the work of MRA.

When one thinks about the fact that by the time Anne was out of the sanatorium the Almonds would have been away from the Arab world for a year, and Basra for two years – their colleagues must have already been scrambling to make other plans for their replacements. Despite this, the Mission Board was very understanding and indeed generous. They paid Anne's medical expenses and the family's eventual passage back to America.

While Anne rested and healed over her months in Leysin, the rest of the family were not inactive. Beverly was living at Caux, looking after baby Betsy with the help of Ellen Kongshaug – a wonderful young Danish woman. There were many others also living at the center out of the summer conference season, so Bev worked with them to take care of the place and its community.

Harry took advantage of this unexpected waiting time to travel with MRA colleagues, especially Francis Goulding (English) and Ismail Hassan (Egyptian), with an interfaith message of change and reconciliation. Harry went to Turkey in Sept. 1951 with Francis; and then was with both men in France in November for the General Assembly of the United Nations, which was convening in Paris. In the spring Harry again traveled with Ismail to Turkey and Lebanon; and then after a brief touch-down in Switzerland, the two of them were off again – this time to America, primarily to the MRA conference in Mackinac Island.

In late June 1952, Anne was happily declared free of TB, and the family was reunited. They had a party on the lawn at Caux, a belated celebration of Betsy's first birthday now the family was all together again. A favorite story Bev tells is when Anne first re-entered her room in Caux and saw her excited baby sister on one bed and a large doll (sent by her Almond grandparents) on the other bed, she was briefly torn between the two. Happily, Betsy, "in her enthusiastic squeals and grins and lunges and hair-pulling soon won hands down." (From a letter written by Bev at the time.)

In the evening of Anne's first day back, when it was time for bed, Bev started to pray in her halting French. Anne said "Maman, je crois qu'il sera mieux si tu prie en Anglais." (Mummy, I think it would be better if you prayed in English!)

Things were not boring for the Almonds at this point as they were helping Anne readapt to family life and to speaking English, and little Betsy was crawling and climbing stairs and getting into everything. They spent a few more months in Caux, partly for Anne to get further mountain air and follow-up care. They then decided it was time for the family to return to America. Not only was there a large and active community of MRA there, but the girls had not yet been there, nor had they ever met their Almond grandparents, nor most of the rest of the family.

CHAPTER 15

Return to the USA

Thus, in Nov. 1952, the family sailed from Le Havre, France on the Holland America Line's ship *Ryndam*, bound for New York City via Halifax, Nova Scotia. Ellen Kongshaug from Denmark, who had already been with the family in Caux, came with them to help with the children. All three adults and Anne were seasick all the way across, while little Betsy, walking by then, felt just fine, which must have created some challenges for her queasy carers.

Met in NYC by Bev's and Harry's parents, the family was offered the use of a house owned by Barclay and Goodie Farr in West Orange, New Jersey. It was a good-sized place, beautifully decorated and furnished as Goodie was a noted professional decorator. The Farrs were family friends, as well as being involved in MRA, and wanted to help. Based there, they were very close to Bloomfield where Harry's parents lived, as well as being near Harry's brother Dick, his wife Grace and their children. This provided the opportunity for the girls to get to know many more of the family. The Prindles, living in Connecticut by then, loaned them a car, so they were well set-up – a generous welcome back home.

It did not take long for Bev and Harry to get fully into the swing of MRA activities back in the USA, and, being an international fellowship, they were often working with friends from other countries whom they had met at Caux or Mackinac in earlier years. In a letter written to the family by Beverly from West Orange on Feb. 23rd, 1953, she describes how Harry had been in Washington, D.C. for a few weeks, and then how she joined him there for some major MRA events. Some quotes from that letter give a sense of the circles in which MRA folk were moving at that time. There was a major meeting at the Shoreham Hotel, preceded by a dinner there for 130 people at which Bev and Harry hosted a table with the Iraqi Ambassador and his wife. "After dinner a meeting for a thousand was held in the Grand Ballroom, and the ambassadors from India, Ceylon, and Japan spoke about what MRA has been doing in their countries – each one spoke differently, sincerely, and convincingly, and it was a great experience to be there and realize that there is hope of banishing the East-West feeling and of having one world, as one of them said." Other speakers included Senator Howard Smith of New Jersey, a recent Korean war veteran, and many others. Bev goes on to describe all the things they did in Washington, and in the days after, during which they seemed to be dashing around New Jersey, into New York City, out to Long Island, and then to the Prindles to help out as Myra was sick – all in a rather breathlessly non-stop manner – classic active Beverly! Presumably the amazing Ellen was looking after the girls in West Orange through all of this whirlwind time.

In the summer of 1953, the whole family went to Mackinac Island and took part in the MRA conference there, and they were then invited to move to an MRA property just north of New York City, which they did at the end of that summer.

The Almonds and Kitchens at Mackinac Island – 1953

Dellwood, the place where the Almonds would live for the next 11 years, was a beautiful estate of 276 acres, an hour's drive north of NYC, in the town of Mount Kisco. It had been owned by Mrs. Emily Hammond, a wealthy widow with links to the Vanderbilt family, who had given it to MRA in 1950 to be used as a gathering place, and as a home for MRA workers. There were six cottages and two much larger houses on the property, along with barns, farm buildings, a tennis court and swimming pool, and many acres of woods and fields.

The Almond family moved into Oak Cottage, a small but very nice home. The house got its name from the stump of what had been a huge oak tree in the yard, about 4 feet across. There were four bedrooms – two tiny ones for Anne and Betsy, a room for Bev and Harry, and one for guests. It must have been a wonderful feeling to be in a house together and settled in the USA, near family and finally able to enjoy some of their wedding gifts and other personal items long stored away.

Oak Cottage was about a 10 minute walk from 'the Big House', the main building on the property. It was about a mile's walk in the other direction from the cottage to the bus stop where Anne would catch her school bus to start kindergarten in the nearby little town of Armonk. Betsy was two at this point and was cared for by Bev or Ellen at home during the day.

Other MRA families lived in the other cottages on the property. Cecil and MJ Broadhurst and their sons Daniel and Joey lived closest to Oak Cottage, just across a field. Dave and Naomi Carey with their children Peter and Susan, and Bob and Joy Amen with sons Robby and John, lived in two other houses a bit further away. Charlie and Betty Brown and their sons lived in yet another cottage. The Bungalow, as the sixth cottage was called, was home to different people over the years, including later on Bev's sister Hope and her husband John Ayer from Canada, who were married in 1957. There were many different people who lived at and helped host the Big House, changing somewhat over time, but with usually one or two couples and a number of single people of various ages. Of all of those at Dellwood, the Careys were particularly good friends, and the family is still in touch with David Carey and his daughter Susan, the childhood friend of Anne and Betsy. David turned 102 in 2015.

Since Dellwood served two main functions, providing a home base for many MRA workers and being a center which could entertain large groups as well as diplomats, business-people and others coming out from NYC, it was always busy. Beverly went to the Big House most days to check in with others there, and to help with entertaining and other needs.

MRA had an office in NYC at 640 Fifth Avenue, to which some people from Dellwood went every day, either driving in or going by train from Mount Kisco. Harry often did this, and Bev went in occasionally as well. The goal was to make contacts in order to help more people know about the philosophy of MRA.

As well as going into NYC and meeting people at the UN, Harry kept in touch with the Arab world and went back there quite often during the family's years at Dellwood. In fact, his first trip began right at the end of 1953, only about four months after the family had settled into Oak Cottage. When the possibility of the trip arose, Harry and Bev explained the plan to the children and together they had some quiet time to reflect on the idea. Anne stated that she would be OK with her Dad going, but only if he promised to send her a postcard from every place he went. Although this might have seemed a simple child's wish at the time, it was taken seriously and the resulting scrapbook, with a map of the itinerary and all the postcards stuck in with their texts written out beside them, is still a precious and useful family keepsake and reference. Harry was in fact gone about five months, leaving Bev and Ellen with the girls, and also the wider Dellwood community as support. See Harry's book for details on this journey.

Throughout the Almonds' Dellwood years, the 1950s and early 1960s, it was a time of great change and upheaval in the Arab world. The establishment of the state of Israel had been a hugely significant factor in 1948, and newly created Arab states were finding their feet and seeking allies to support them. The Cold War tugged back and forth in this region with both sides trying to woo the Arab nations with promises of development aid and support. The Suez Canal was fought over and much else was going on. Harry continued to keep abreast of these issues with visits to the region several times, as well as keeping in contact with various Arab personalities at the United Nations in New York.

On some occasions Bev traveled with Harry. In 1955 they revisited Iraq, and they also spent time in Egypt to make arrangements for a large MRA international group performing the musical show *The Vanishing Island* which was touring around the world. This show had been invited by government leaders in various countries. In Cairo the entire group was received by President Nasser, and later in Iran by the Shah. Over the next few years, Harry also visited Lebanon, Algeria, and Morocco, sometimes more than once.

Because the family were at Dellwood and part of the MRA community there, they always had support to care for the girls as needed when both parents were away. Bev's parents, the Kitchens, stayed with them several times; and her sister Hope and husband, John Ayer, at other times. When family wasn't available, there were other people who were already good friends and part of the community that stepped up to help; creative, caring people such as Anna Hale (first met in Caux in 1952), and Margaret Schwab from Connecticut, whose whole family were good friends, and whose youngest sister Irene was a special friend of Anne's.

The family with their beloved dog, Briar, in 1958 at Dellwood

For myself as a child, I (Anne) remember Dellwood as a fabulous place to grow up. There were lots of other kids around, endless woods and fields to explore on our own; cows, pigs, and dogs on the farm; fascinating people to meet from around the world, and some wonderful people who helped look after us as mentioned above. Margaret Schwab taught us how to ice skate on the pond in the woods, and her sister Edith gave us piano lessons. Anna Hale taught us how to swim in the pool on the property, took us camping and on many other adventures, and was an extraordinary story-teller. We were taken several summers by Anna and others to a beautiful beach house on Long Island Sound that had been loaned for the use of MRA kids, and so we had what amounted to our own private summer camp there.

I remember meeting German coal miners, Japanese students, a Buddist abbot from Thailand, a Japanese opera singer who had the same birthday as me, and a steady stream of other fascinating people from around the world. As we got a little older, we were sometimes asked to help with cooking or serving meals for such visitors, and that was usually interesting too. I clearly remember toasting seaweed sheets over a flame and making little rice balls which we wrapped in the seaweed for the Japanese student group to enjoy. We also got involved at various times in helping with mail-outs of MRA books or information, and I remember that as a time of working with a team of friends on what we felt was an important project.

There was usually lots going on at Dellwood which included not just those who lived there or those who visited from afar, but others in the area who were involved in MRA. The Morris and Schwab families from Connecticut (CT), and the Hodges from New Jersey, all had daughters around our ages who were good friends. I am in touch with several of them still today. The family of actor Sidney Poitier came on several occasions to visit, as did the then wife of Anthony Quinn and their daughter Vallie, who became a friend of Betsy's. We also got to know the Close family from Greenwich, CT, who later moved to Dellwood for some time. Their second daughter, Glenn (the actress),

RETURN TO THE USA

was a friend, as was the youngest daughter, Jessie; and the Close's two Shetland ponies were a very popular addition to life there for all of us kids.

Having said all that, as an adult looking back now I see it a bit differently. I am still very grateful for the childhood I had, but realize that there was much going on that I didn't fully grasp until much later. MRA, like much of the USA, was very involved in the Cold War mentality and thus often very anti-Communist. Perhaps it was this 'ideological thinking' that had MRA people seeing themselves as revolutionary world-changers and thus putting pressure on themselves or others to behave in certain ways.

Beverly certainly remembers that there was a hierarchy within the organization with leaders and followers, and she gives an amusing but also rather telling example of this. "We felt that the leaders' opinions did carry weight. At one point, when seamless stockings came in, they somehow were not considered good or proper, so when finally we found that one of the 'leaders' was wearing seamless stockings, we felt we could wear them too. I mean, stuff like that is so unbelievable now."

Beverly remembers that she and Harry visited another couple at Dellwood to challenge them about some personal marital issues, and that later they regretted their manner of interference deeply, to the extent of apologizing to them for this some 10-15 years later when they met up again. There was certainly an attitude of intense self-examination to perhaps an unhealthy extreme at times, and a similarly intense challenging of others. Beverly now also regrets how little the Dellwood folk got involved in the local community, and feels that their distance may have created a mystery about the place and what was going on there. That was probably reflective of both a sense of self-sufficiency by the Dellwood folk, and the feeling that they were too busy 'changing the world' on the wider stage to be much involved in local matters.

Nevertheless, as mentioned before, many deep, caring friendships developed during this time for Bev and Harry, and some of them continued for years, even to the present.

Such friends included John Newington, a businessman in Greenwich, CT, and his wife Barbara. John and Harry shared a passion for sailing, and Harry spent many happy hours with John on his yacht *Serena* in Long Island Sound.

In the late 50s, probably 1958 or 1959, John Newington learned of an upcoming conference of Arab leaders scheduled for Cairo. Harry was urged to go, both by Newington and by Dr. A. K. Hassouna, Secretary General of the Arab League, who was also a friend. In fact, Newington offered to pay the costs for Harry and another man to go. But for whatever reason, Harry's MRA colleagues rebuffed this plan, and no one from MRA went. Harry was hurt and angry and felt that others had spread misinformation about the trip to undercut him. Sadly, he retreated from his conviction for the Arab world for a time. Beverly and the girls remember this as the time when the family dog, Briar (named after Bev's childhood dog), had a fancy dog house built for him by a disgruntled Harry needing to find something to do! He also decided that at least he could help MRA by working on boats, which he knew well, and he did that at the conference center on Mackinac Island for the next few years.

During the winter of 1959-1960 MRA built a film studio on the island, and Harry drove the barge bringing over supplies – a grueling task in the ice and winter storms of the Great Lakes. Bev and the girls joined him there for Christmas, 1959. Those long cold nights at the helm of that barge gave Harry lots of time to reflect, and although he helped out with the boats for the next few summers at Mackinac, he re-found his passionate concern for the Arab world, kept himself informed on the issues, and waited to see how the next opportunity to serve there might come.

CHAPTER 16

Beirut - back to the Arab world

In 1963, Harry received a letter from the former President of Lebanon, Alfred Naccache, inviting him and his family to move to Beirut, Lebanon to be a liason for the Arab world with the work of MRA. The letter meant much to Harry and Bev, confirming their convictions about the Arab world. This time the Almonds' colleagues fully supported them in their decision. So once again the family began to pack up, ready to return to the Middle East.

Lebanon is a small country, at the eastern end of the Mediterranean, bordered by Syria on the north and east and by Israel on the south. This puts it right in the midst of the many controversies that have swept over the Middle East from ancient times to the present. It is a beautiful country, with a narrow coastal plain rising up into tall mountains, capped with snow for many months of the year, and home of the famed cedars of Lebanon. To the east of the Lebanon Range is the lush Bekaa Valley, an area of rich agriculture as well as ancient sites, most notably the city of

Baalbeck. The far side of the valley rises into the Anti-Lebanon Range, where there is the border with Syria. Lebanon has been a trading crossroads and center of commerce and banking for centuries, if not millennia, and so is called by many the 'Switzerland of the Middle East'. The fact that it was a French mandate for many years also helps make it cosmopolitan, and means that many there speak Arabic, French, and English. Lebanon has several universities and other cultural resources such as the Baalbeck Festival. It was to this fascinating part of the world that the Almonds headed, and once again a new home for the family.

Harry went ahead to Beirut in March, 1964 to prepare, and was joined there by an old friend and MRA colleague from earlier Mid East travels, Hansjorg Gareis of Germany. The ladies of the family followed in the summer, once school was out, to join Harry in the apartment he had found. He had enrolled the girls in the Lebanese Evangelical School for Girls (LESG), where Anne (now 16) would go into the senior class, Form VI, and Betsy (aged 13) would go into Form III. Run by British missionaries, with only girl students, and uniforms, it was quite a change from the public schools of the USA; but both girls made friends and had good experiences there. After attending for one year and graduating from LESG, Anne moved on to do a B.A. in education at the Beirut College for Women. Betsy continued at LESG until her graduation in 1968.

For the first few years the Almonds lived in an apartment on Sharia Madhat Pasha, a street in a Muslim neighborhood near the Sanaya Gardens and the girls' school. From the balcony there was a distant but clear view of the snow-capped mountains for which the country is named. (Laban/lebnah is from the Arabic root word for milk or white.) The family in the large old villa across the street kept pigeons in their garden, and the view of the city often included that flock of birds swirling around the rooftops.

One memorable feature of life there was the pushcart vendors with fruit, vegetables, roast corn, or chestnuts, who would come along the street crying out their wares. If there were items to be purchased, a lively and loud discussion would ensue between street and balcony, and a basket with money in it would be lowered on a rope to purchase the goods that were then hauled back up. The apartment was also near a mosque, and the regular melodic calls to prayer were a backdrop to life, as were the reminders to 'rise and shine' during the month of Ramadan in order to cook and eat before sunrise on each day of fasting.

Later the family moved to a larger home, a villa they rented from the Mejdalani family, also in west Beirut, which gave space for larger groups to gather and more guests to stay. Several memories of that house remain clear: the jasmine that was growing on the iron work of the windows and which scented our rooms at night, the wild cats in the neighborhood that tried to get in at every opportunity and howled loudly many nights, the flat roof where we had lines to dry our laundry, and the wonderful Palestinian woman, Rosa Khalaf, who came to help with cleaning and laundry and also introduced us to the delicious rice and lentil dish called mujedderah, the same dish called a 'mess of pottage' by Esau in the Bible.

Rosa was an important part of laundry day, when the washing machine was rolled up to the sink and then needed hoses hooked up to put water in and drain it out. There were two tubs in this machine, one for washing and rinsing, and one for spinning the water out. Then the wet clothes had to be fished out of the wash side to go into the spin side. The damp clothes were then carried to the roof to be hung on lines to dry – all quite a complex and fascinating operation.

Also lingering in family memory are the few times that Beverly tried to practice her written Arabic by writing the grocery list for the nearby neighborhood market. Someone would be dispatched to drop off the list, and occasionally some of the items later delivered bore little or no resemblance to what she thought she had ordered! Whether it was her Arabic handwriting or the wrong word written, wasn't clear, but she was teased about this by her family.

When asked about what she remembers and enjoyed from Beirut, Beverly, typically, answers, "The people – we made quite a few friends there." There were those met at the American Church and in other organizations, and neighbors from the apartment building including the Everests, an English family – Kate and Jack and their two young boys. Jack was a pilot for Kuwait Airways. There were friends from Harry's earlier visits, and also people they'd known elsewhere who had moved there, such as the Luiden family from Basra. Amazingly, they also reconnected with Mohammed Yassir, around whom the controversy had swirled in Bahrain many years before. The Nakib family, old friends from Basra, were also now in Lebanon with their four children, one of whom was at college with Anne. Nedko and Aznive Etinoff (originally from Bulgaria) and the Derderians (Armenians) were two MRA-connected families whom Harry had met on his earlier trips to Beirut and who became good family friends.

Bev was involved with the American Women's Club (AWC). "We supported various local craftspeople such as glassblowers, weavers, potters, etc., and we had fairs and festivals for them. The ladies of the club would go around the countryside to find craftspeople and get them to participate in the fairs to promote their wares." Beverly became second Vice President of the Club in charge of service projects.

This photo was taken in the Sanayeh Garden in Beirut and shows Beverly with (LtoR): Mrs. Dwight Porter, the American Ambassador's wife; Mrs. Middleton, AWC; Dr. Issam Haidar – Director General of the Ministry of Youth and Sports; and Mr. Melham Sulman, also from the Ministry. This was on the occasion of the AWC handing over to the Ministry the Volunteer Recreation Program they had gotten started in this park.

A favorite pastime for the family most weekends was to go off into the countryside on expeditions to explore the many and varied historic and ancient sites, and to walk and picnic in the gorgeous mountainous countryside. Invariably, a local child would spot us, go tell his friends, and then we'd find ourselves under careful observation by what Harry liked to call "the local branch of the foreigner viewing society."

At the same time, in the city were modern shops and anything a person could want was for sale. One popular 'take-out' family meal was schwarma (grilled meat wrap-style sandwiches) from the little shops across from the American University of Beirut not far from our house.

Another element that affected the Almonds' time in Beirut was that a new MRA conference center opened in Panchgani, India in 1967. Many MRA people from Europe traveled to take part in conferences there, and these colleagues soon discovered that a stop in Beirut was an easy and pleasant way to break the journey. This also gave Harry and Bev the chance to introduce Lebanese folk interested in MRA to an array of people from different countries who had experience applying the principles in their lives and work.

During their years in Beirut, Harry and Bev wrote a regular newsletter to people around the Middle East who had expressed interest in the work of MRA, in which they shared stories and news of events and conferences around the world. They held many meetings, receptions and meals at their home, as well as meeting with all sorts of people in their homes and offices around the country.

Marcel and Theri Grandy were a Swiss couple living on the island of Cyprus, also working with MRA. They were not only the Almonds' nearest colleagues, but became their closest friends. There were many visits back and forth in collaboration with them, as Cyprus was a short flight from Beirut. The Almonds went to the Caux conferences every summer while they lived in Lebanon, so became much more connected with Swiss and other European MRA colleagues.

Harry and Beverly while visiting Cyprus in the late 1960s

Other MRA friends came to Lebanon to stay for longer periods and work with Beverly and Harry. One such friend was Dr. Charis Waddy, the first woman to get a degree in Semitic languages from Oxford, and a delightful personality. As well as her academic interest, she had lived in Jerusalem as a child when her father, Canon Waddy, was chaplain to General Allenby of the British Army during WWI, and had helped establish St. George's Anglican Cathedral there. Visiting such sites as the ancient city of Byblos with Charis was a unique adventure as she could and would stop to read the inscriptions carved into the stones on various ruins and tell us all about it. Charis re-ignited her earlier love of the Arab and Muslim world while living in Beirut at this time, then wrote a book called *Baalbeck Caravans*, and later several other books, especially about women in the Muslim world.

Betsy and Anne remember coming home from school one day, when Harry and Bev were away leaving Charis in charge, to find her sitting on the stairs outside the apartment door. She had gone out to get something, the door had locked behind her so she couldn't get in, but she'd known school would be out soon, and the girls would be back with a key, so didn't worry. What a delightful and interesting person she was, and a good friend indeed.

Charis and another British friend, Mary Rowlatt, were part of a special family adventure in the spring of 1965. Mary had grown up in Cairo and so was fluent in Arabic, and her family had been active with the Oxford Group/MRA in Cairo in the 1930s. These two and the four Almonds set off from Beirut in a mini-van to visit friends in Jordan and Jerusalem and to see some of the holy sites. This took place in April 1965, thus well before the Six-Day war of 1967 when boundaries changed. Given that Beverly wrote her family a four-page typed letter to describe the trip, and then apologized for not giving more detail, only a few highlights will be included here.

They drove east through the mountains of Lebanon, into the Bekaa Valley, over the Anti-Lebanon range and on to Damascus, the capital of Syria. Later they stopped to tour the Roman city of Jerash, just north of Amman, Jordan, where they spent the night and the next day seeing friends. Then west and down to the ancient city of Jericho, a picnic lunch by the Dead Sea, and up into the hills again to Jerusalem. Given that this was the week after Easter, the area was full of visitors, and so they stayed in a small family-run hotel in Ramullah, just north of Jerusalem. The four days there were filled with a rich mix of visiting old friends and significantly older sites – such as the Church of the Holy Sepulcher, the Dome of the Rock, and the Temple Mount. Certainly for all of them, seeing these special places familiar from the Bible was a precious and unique experience.

The group then headed further south to another ancient place, the city of Petra in southern Jordan, again a once-in-a-lifetime experience. The car was left at the Rest House near Petra, and then everyone had to put their bags on a donkey and ride horses to the destination. Quite the sight, as Bev describes it: "Charis wearing plaid flannel trousers borrowed from a neighbor in Beirut, Mary in jodphurs, and me in an extra pair of Betsy's blue jeans – we really were glamorous. We rode down through a deep canyon called the Siq surrounded by rocks on both sides for half an hour. It is the only way to get into the ancient 'Rose-red City' of Petra which was built by the Nabateans somewhere between 650 and 300 B.C." Finally one emerges around a corner to be faced with a vast monumental building carved into the reddish sandstone right before you. And that was only the first of many amazing structures to be seen in this magical spot. Bev continues, "We settled into our 'rooms' – again caves carved out of the rock, but actual rooms with doors and 2 cots and a table in each." That afternoon and the next morning, after a night sleeping in the caves, we explored the wonders of the place; including Aaron's tomb on Mount Hor, led around by local guides. After all that, back to Amman, and then home to Beirut the next day – an amazing and unforgettable week for all.

One of the more dramatic periods of the Almond Beirut experience was in early June, 1967, during the 'Six Day War'[5]. Harry describes this well in his book. "The US embassy officer responsible for our district telephoned to inform us that we were to report in two hours at the athletic field of the American University of Beirut. From there a Marine guard would escort us to the airport to board special planes that would take us either to Rome, Nicosia, Athens, or Ankara. For this evacuation we would be permitted one suitcase each. I thanked him and said we would call back.

"It was June 6, Betsy's 16th birthday, and a cake was in the oven. We prayed for guidance as to whether or not to accept the embassy's offer. After a quiet moment or two we each had a similar thought: it was God who had brought us here, and we should not leave until it was clear that He meant for us to leave. So I called back to the embassy. It was difficult to get through to the vice-consul who had called us earlier, and the line was very noisy. When he came on line, he said, 'You sure picked a helluva time to call: we're under attack'. The vice-consul made it clear that if we didn't leave, the embassy could no longer assume any responsibility for our safety. We stayed.

"The only damage done was to Betsy's birthday cake: it burned in the oven, forgotten in the excitement. There were fears of an Israeli air attack, and we had to black out our windows. We stayed indoors for three days. We did not even show our faces on our fifth floor balcony for fear of the mobs flowing down our narrow street. They filled it from wall to wall, pouring over parked cars like a

5 This war, that lasted from June 5-10, 1967, was the time when Israel seized the West Bank, Gaza, the Golan Heights, and the Sinai Peninsula by roundly defeating the Arab forces of Egypt, Jordan and Syria.

stream of locusts. We were fortunately living in a Muslim neighborhood where Americans did not normally stay, but the mobs destroyed the nearby PanAm offices and attacked American cars, regardless of who owned them.

"The Nakibs (our old friends from Basra) drove a big American Ford, fire engine red. Ahmed was in Europe when the war occurred, but Sajida (his wife) and her son Hisham came to find out if we were safe or needed anything. Sajida seemed a bit nervous as she sat down. Hisham told us that when they were parking their car a few men had demanded in a rough manner to know who owned 'the American car'. Sajida, a diminutive lady, drew herself up to full aristocratic dignity and said, 'It belongs to Ahmed bin Hamid Al-Nakib, and it's none of your business!' They half-bowed apologetically and disappeared. Hisham asked if he could get us any provisions. We said we had plenty of food, thanks, but that it would be great if he could fetch our mail from our downtown post office box, which he kindly did."

During those days of the war, one of Betsy's school friends (with a Muslim Lebanese father) came with her parents and brought us a big bag of groceries, and we were also visited by a Christian Lebanese friend who wanted to be sure we were alright. Other Lebanese friends called and made comments along the lines of, "Oh you're still here, good. We were afraid you might have left with the other Americans." Later on it began to seem like the Almonds were the only Americans who hadn't left, but in any case, Lebanese friends appreciated what the family had done, had more confidence in the Almonds' commitment to the area, and felt able to more freely express their feelings about America as well.

While Harry and Beverly were in Beirut, many things were changing with MRA in America, and the Almonds were concerned about these changes, and the apparent narrowing of focus to being just on youth and a development called "Up With People". (See Appendix for more information on these changes.) Financial backing for the Almonds and their work from America dried up, and the family were not sure how to continue with what they felt called to do in the Middle East. There was one day in 1966 when Harry was so concerned about their finances that he went to the Dean at the American University of Beirut and asked about the possibility of getting a job there. When he got home he learned that not only had a generous check arrived from a Dutch MRA friend, with the promise of more to come regularly, but that Anne had been given a full merit scholarship by her college to continue her studies. Other friends in Europe also began to provide support that kept the family going, and reinforced their certainty about what they were doing in Lebanon.

Over time, more and more Lebanese people got involved and took on a commitment for their country, above religion or other affiliations. One of these was Ramez Salameh, a law student when first met by the Almonds, now an experienced lawyer, who with many others continues to the present day to work for the future of the country through all the turmoil and fighting of the past years, and to build bridges across sectarian divides.

Another such person is Assaad Chaftari, who in November 2014 wrote a wonderful letter to Beverly: "I write to you from a very troubled Lebanon and Middle East where violence and division prevail for the moment being. But you also know that there are very active teams of the MRA Group in Palestine, Egypt, Lebanon, Tunisia, and two very active persons too in Syria working against the stream to promote personal change, moral values, dialogue and love. Although it is not always obvious but this work is somehow one of the fruits of the long years your couple and many others have so generously given to our countries and people to spread the teaching of Mr. Frank Buchman. It really needed also

Absolute Love and Unselfishness to leave everything behind and serve our area's people, and a lot of courage. Mrs. Almond, I need to express through this late letter my deep gratitude to you and the late Reverend Harry because your legacy is what keeps us going everyday. Your example and perseverance is what is showing us the north." (This is a reference to the 'true north' or 'right direction'.) These words meant a great deal to Beverly. Although recognition was never the goal of their work – it was deeply touching to receive this confirmation that they had indeed left a strong legacy which continues decades later.

It should be added that Israelis and Palestinians committed to reconciliation have been to the Caux conference center several times over the years, and keep in touch with each other and with MRA people in other parts of the world.

Harry and Beverly lived in Lebanon until 1972, although the girls had left before that to travel with a European-based MRA musical show called "Anything to Declare" (ATD). The cast was composed largely of younger people, most from Europe, who offered what they felt they had to 'declare' to the world in terms of stories of people bringing change to various situations, all portrayed in skits and musical numbers. Betsy joined the cast in 1968 when she graduated from high school, while the show was touring in Europe. After graduating from college, Anne joined the group a year later, when the show was preparing to travel to Asia and Australasia. Harry and Beverly connected with this group twice – once over Christmas 1969 at the MRA center in India, and again when they helped prepare for and shepherd ATD's visit to Iran in April, 1971.

It was the Almonds' 25th wedding anniversary in 1971, and they celebrated it in unexpected style in Caux. Two Lebanese girls, Maha and Miriam Dib, the daughters of Butros Dib, the Secretary to the Office of the President in Lebanon, had been sent by their parents with the Almonds to Caux for part of the summer. Because the Dib girls were there, the former President of Lebanon, Charles Helou, and his wife, decided to visit them and Caux. The Dib and Almond girls together cooked a wonderful Lebanese meal for the Helous, which also celebrated Harry and Bev's anniversary – quite a special time.

At this point, Harry and Beverly began to feel that they had fulfilled their goal of passing on the torch to a group of Lebanese people, and that it was time to go home. During these years in Lebanon, Harry's father had died, and he had flown home to conduct the service. Now, Bev and Harry felt it was time to be closer to their remaining parents and the rest of the family.

CHAPTER 17

Home Again

The four Almonds came back to the US together in the fall of 1971, and spent the first weeks visiting family in the New York/New Jersey area, and in Kansas where Harry's brother Dick and his family were. They then had a wonderful Christmas in Missouri with Bev's parents, sister Hope, her husband John Ayer, and their two children Aaron and Victoria, who had both been born while the Almonds were in Beirut, and were now 5 and 3 years old. Beverly remembers that despite the cold of a December day, " . . . when we arrived at their farm – those kids came running out in bare feet in their excitement to greet us!"

As well as being a precious reunion for all the family, the time with the Ayers also brought a reconnection for Beverly with her sister Hope. Looking back, Bev realizes how little time the two of them had spent together. In fact she said, "We didn't really grow up together." What with being seven years apart in age, then going off to different boarding schools, and the different travels that both of them had done through the intervening years, they hadn't seen very much of each other. Therefore this Christmas time was very special.

Christmas 1971 in Cabool, Missouri
Back: Betsy, Harry, Bev, Hope and John. Center: Vic and
Elsie seated. Victoria, Anne and Aaron in front.

The decade or so following the Almonds' return to America
proved to be a time of many challenging transitions; involving
moves in and out of many different homes, changes of all kinds
on the family front, and also much going on with the efforts to re-
establish the wider work of MRA in the USA.

After that family Christmas, the four Almonds went to a conference in Quebec, Canada over New Year 1972, which was part
of the process of re-building MRA in North America. Following
that, Bev and Harry travelled a great deal in both Canada and the
US in 1972-73, in order to talk with former colleagues about this
re-building process.

Eventually, they based for some months with Bev's sister Myra and her family in Redding, Connecticut. During this time, in October 1973, Anne got married to Bryan Hamlin from England, whom she had gotten to know in Quebec the previous year. The family shared a happy Christmas in Connecticut in 1973, and then the newlyweds moved to western Canada, and the Almonds to an apartment in Bloomfield, New Jersey, close to Harry's Mom. Betsy, meanwhile, had returned to London to work with MRA there.

The Almonds' home in New Jersey proved a good place from which to travel around the continent, and for Harry to go into New York City where an office for the transitioning MRA work was located. Later they moved into NYC where they stayed in various different places short term, and eventually into a property purchased by MRA.

All of these moves of Harry and Bev paralleled the upheavals going on with the work to which they had given their lives. Over the span of several years in the mid-70s, negotiations went on between the still-existing old MRA board (primarily supporting Up With People), and the group, including Harry and Bev, that wanted to reclaim the name for the wider vision they held. (See Appendix for more detail.) Beverly recalls that it was a very difficult time, with "anger and tears, and we were divided from old friends with whom we had worked closely for years." Finally, in the summer of 1976, agreements were made, the MRA board was reconstituted with a majority of new members, and Harry became Executive Director of the board of this revitalized MRA in America.

As always, the Almonds continued to carry the Arab and Muslim world in their hearts, and they made friends in those communities in New York. Beverly became a member of the Islamic Heritage Society, an organization composed of women from the various Muslim countries' diplomatic groups in the city. It welcomed non-Muslims warmly, and organized regular informative meetings about social and cultural topics. At the Society's annual dinner, Beverly and Harry sat with Parwin Zikria, an Afghan, and her surgeon husband Bashir. The two couples became good friends and remained so over many years.

Meanwhile many changes were occurring within the family as well. In 1976, following the reconstitution of MRA USA, Anne and Bryan returned from Canada to live in the US, and based in the Boston area. Soon after that, Betsy was engaged to Rob Lancaster from Australia. They too were working with MRA, and after their wedding in New York in June, 1977, they based at and hosted the MRA center there.

In early 1975, Beverly's father was in very poor health, and Bev was able to go and spend some time with him, her mother, and the Ayers. She was there when he died in late January at the Ayer home in Missouri, a sad but precious time together. Many of the family gathered to celebrate his nearly 84 years of life at the Smith Meeting House Cemetery in Gilmanton in August of that year. There was a simple service, conducted by Harry, and Vic's ashes were interred in the Kitchen family plot. Elsie came east for this service and then spent some time with her daughters Beverly and Myra. Tragically, Myra died suddenly at age 55 in June the following year, so the family again gathered in Gilmanton to remember her. This was a hard period for Myra's children, and all the extended Kitchen family.

Finally, in early 1977, the Almonds acquired a small house of their own in Falls Village, Connecticut, the very first house they had ever owned. It was a simple little red wooden house right on the banks of the Housatonic River, originally built as a summer place. The previous owner had been the actor Hal Holbrook, best known for his portrayals of Mark Twain. At first it was used by the Almonds and others as a get-away spot from the city, but over time the Almonds based there more and more. It was high time that Bev and Harry had a place they could call home. Meanwhile,

Elsie continued to come east from Missouri each summer and visit Beverly and the rest of the family.

This is how Bev described the Falls Village story when interviewed in 2015. "Harry and I were staying at a friend's place in Connecticut for a time, and Harry was out looking around at houses as we thought it was time to get our own place. One day he came back and said 'I think I've found the place!' So we went together and we both liked it and felt it was the place we wanted. The house was bought in the spring of 1977, and Rob and Betsy actually spent their honeymoon there that June."

Even after purchasing this home in the country, the Almonds were in and out of NYC, especially when Rob and Betsy went to Zimbabwe for a year in 1980-81. Once the Lancasters were back in the States, Rob suggested that it was time that Elsie stopped going back and forth across the continent, and that she ought to come and live in the East, where most of her relatives were. He promised Bev that he would help look after her. "Which he did – he was very good about that," says Bev. Eventually, the Almonds built an additional room for Elsie, and later added a big room for grandchildren upstairs.

Harry and Bev with their mothers at Falls Village, 1983

During the Falls Village years, Harry's mother also visited often and in fact celebrated her 95th birthday with many of the family there in 1985. She had been living in Bloomfield, NJ for many years with her youngest sister, Alys; but then it became too much for Alys to care for her. The Almonds arranged an ambulance, and Bev rode with her mother-in-law from New Jersey to a nursing home near Falls Village in Canaan, CT – not a fun or easy trip for anyone. Mom Almond died there some months later, in May, 1986, when she was 96 years old.

But the changes in the family also included joyous ones. Anne and Bryan, now living in Cambridge, Massachusetts, gave the Almonds their first grandchild, Rebecca, born in November, 1978. Three years later the Lancasters had a son Christopher, born in March, 1982; and the Hamlins' second child, John, was born just 10 days later. Jennifer Lancaster came along in October, 1984, and these four grandchildren brought lots of happiness to Harry and Bev in the years that followed.

Despite caring for both mothers during the years based in Falls Village, the Almonds made a couple of trips back to the Middle East along with their Swiss friends Marcel and Theri Grandy. Together they visited Cyprus, Turkey, Lebanon, and Jordan in the spring of 1979. They also went several more times to the MRA conferences in Switzerland.

With Elsie living in the Falls Village home, someone had to be around to help her, so Bev was generally based more at home. Both Anne and Betsy and their husbands would come and stay at times, as did other relatives and several good friends.

Recollecting their Falls Village years Beverly said, "We were active in the Congregational Church there; we met Bob Duebber, the pastor, who became a very dear friend. We did go into NYC fairly often. We were not terribly involved in the community, except for the church, but we did make some life-long friends there."

Bev got involved in the DAR[6] during that period as well. "While we were in Falls Village, Father saw something in the newspaper about the DAR, and we knew that Dot Chinatti whom we had met at church belonged to it, and Father said to me 'you're eligible to join, why don't you talk to Dot?' That's how I joined – I got in the easy way, I signed up through my grandmother who had been a member. Now you have to go through such hoops, and it's so expensive to join. But there again, in the DAR I've made some good friends.

"And then we got flooded out. We had been thinking the house was too small. What with Mother there, there wasn't much room for guests, except the big room upstairs where the grandchildren slept. Flooding was what helped us decide about this. One spring it flooded so much that we couldn't drive in. We had to row across the back yard and then walk up the path to the road. Our friends George and Elsie Freeman took mother in, and a local couple – he was first selectman and a retired state policeman – took Harry and me in until we could get back into the house again. The water flooded into the house itself, and the bottom drawers of things were all soaked. Someone came and sorted out all the papers and things in those bottom drawers and dried them out for us. A lot of people helped us then, and the Red Cross was very good too. So we knew we had to move.

"Somewhere along the line, Lilian Lancaster, son-in-law Rob's mother from Australia, came to visit. She and Rob drove around the area looking, and they found this house in Egremont, Massachusetts. We moved here in 1986. Harry and I went to Caux

6 The DAR is the Daughters of the American Revolution, an organization whose members are women who have ancestors that fought for independence during this war. They support the study of history and give scholarships for that, as well as preserving and marking historic sites.

that summer, and Anne stayed with Mother. She called us in Caux on our wedding anniversary, and said 'I have a good present for you, the Falls Village house has sold'."

When granddaughter Rebecca (then 8) heard that the house in Falls Village was being sold, she burst into tears and said, "But I've been coming here all my life!" Bev and Harry had lived 9 years there, so all of the family had wonderful memories of that place.

Christmas 1984 at the home in Falls Village – all the family
Back left are Elsie Kitchen and Millard Almond – the Grandmas!
Back right are Harry, with baby Jennifer Lancaster on his lap, and Beverly
Left – Bryan, Anne, John Hamlin with Rebecca in
front.   Right – Betsy, Christopher and Rob Lancaster

CHAPTER 18

Baldwin Hill

When the Almonds made the move to Egremont, Massachusetts in 1986 they were both 68 years old. Their new house was on Baldwin Hill in North Egremont, about 45 minutes drive north of Falls Village, and fairly equidistant from Boston and NYC, where their two daughters lived with their families. Happily it was up on a hill, so flooding would not be an issue again! This would turn out to be the place they would live longer than anywhere else in either of their lives.

Beverly remembers: "Mother moved with us, she was in the room that is now mine, we were in the room that became Father's office, and he had a study in the basement. The corner room has always been the guest room.

"The very first morning, after we'd spent our first night here, mid-morning the doorbell rang and there was the Rev. Jim Chase, welcoming us to Egremont. His daughter had been renting the downstairs apartment so he knew the house. That was so moving, and he and his wife Helen became life-long friends.

"Bit by bit we began to get involved. How I ever got on the Finance Committee of the town, knowing as little as I do about finances, I can't imagine, but I was the secretary. I was on the Finance Committee with Micky Blanco, and Harry was on the Board of Health with George Blanco, so we got to know them quite soon. And then Harry was on various other committees, so we became quickly involved in the community". They also decided to join the Congregational Church in nearby Great Barrington, and certainly made many good friends there.

Regarding Harry's involvement with the fire department, "It might even have been Jim Chase who said, 'One thing that unites the town is the fire department'. I don't know if Jim had been chaplain, but anyway, Harry soon became chaplain of the Fire Department. He took it quite seriously and would always go to fires and other emergencies." Harry kept the police scanner on at home and would hear right away if there was an emergency and go dashing off to help out at all times of the day or night.

Beverly joined the League of Women Voters after moving to Egremont, and she and Harry also became very engaged in the community through their natural interest in and care for people; taking a loaf of bread to welcome new neighbors, inviting people for meals, and so on. Of course family continued to be a big part of life, and both daughters and their husbands came to Egremont frequently with their children for holidays and special family occasions.

Grandma Elsie, called GG by her great-grandchildren, enjoyed being part of all the flow of visitors and family activity, and a large group of relatives gathered for a "Rollicking Rodman Reunion" to celebrate Elsie's 95th birthday in 1988 – Rodman being Elsie's maiden name. Beverly looked after her wonderfully, in later years with the help of occasional visiting nurses. It was a big factor of life for the Almonds for those years to have her living with them. Finally, in the fall of 1989, they made the decision, very painful for Bev, to move Elsie to a nearby nursing home where she could get full-time care. Bev visited her there daily and also befriended many other residents, becoming in effect part of that community herself during her mother's time there.

Elsie died at that nursing home in Dec. 1991, just a few months before her 99th birthday. Once again, in August 1992, the whole family gathered in Gilmanton, at the Smith Meeting House Cemetery, to celebrate her amazing long and full life. Beverly and Hope were there with their husbands, children, and extended family, and all five of the Prindle grandchildren with their families too.

Beverly remembers that one of her mother's frequent sayings was "Rain before seven, sun before eleven", and adds, "It was raining that morning, but it was clear by the time we were in the cemetery, the sun was out!"

When asked for her thoughts about her mother, Beverly said, "We were always very close, really like best friends. We could and did talk to each other about anything. It was very special." So this was the end of an era – the last of the parents' generation to go.

Another challenge came a few years later when Bev's sister Hope was diagnosed with breast cancer in the mid-1990s. She had a radical mastectomy and then was deemed fully cured. *Note from Anne: I will always remember how Aunt Hopie, while visiting my parents at one point after this experience, offered, in fact almost insisted, on showing some of us women her mastectomy scar, which she did. She really felt we should understand and not be scared of such things, and I really appreciated that, although it was hard at the time. The courage of those Kitchen sisters continued strong.*

During the years in Falls Village, but even more so in Egremont, Harry did a lot of writing: a booklet of devotions called "Foundations for Faith"; *Iraqi Statesman*, the biography of Fadhel Jamali, the former Foreign Minister and a good friend; and finally Harry's own story, *An American in the Middle East*, which has been referred to and quoted several times in this book.

1996 was an exciting year for the family. It was Bev and Harry's 50th wedding anniversary, it was the 50th anniversary of the Caux conference center, Rebecca graduated from high school and headed off to college, and, of all things, while Bev and Harry were in Kansas visiting his brother Dick, a tornado hit Great Barrington and Egremont and did some serious damage, but luckily for them, not to their home. On their anniversary in August, the family gathered and celebrated this special pair – including organizing a game of ping-pong to commemorate the shipboard game that had first brought them together! There was a banner on the front lawn announcing the occasion to all passers-by, and a mystery trip leading to a special dinner out for all the family.

There are so many stories from this period that could be told about Bev's fun-loving spirit. For example, at some point in the early Egremont years, a number of the family, including Beverly, decided to go on a hike over Jug End, along part of the Appalachian Trail. Harry, not so physically adventurous as his wife, dropped off the hikers at the trailhead and a pick-up point was agreed upon. When the group emerged hours later onto the road, however, there was no sign of Harry. In those pre-cellphone days, there wasn't much they could do, so it was decided to try and hitch a ride. The first vehicle that stopped was a pick-up truck, and before anyone knew what was happening, Bev was scrambling into the back of it – so of course the others followed her example, chuckling in amazement as she was in her 70s at the time.

2000 was a tough year as Harry's brother Dick died of cancer in Kansas, and then in the fall Bev broke her shoulder when she tripped and fell. The local doctors felt she should go to Boston to get replacement surgery done, and so she and Harry spent several weeks with the Hamlins; first waiting for the surgery, and then while Bev was at Spaulding Rehab to get her shoulder moving again. A classic Beverly moment occurred when Anne was helping her mother take a bath one day. Both were quite struck by the large rainbow array of bruises around the broken shoulder, and Bev suddenly asked, "Do you want to take a picture of it?" That photo was not taken, but both had a good laugh!

Another delightful moment occurred at John's graduation from Bates College in Maine in 2004. Bev attended the event, and none of the Hamlins will ever forget seeing Rebecca teaching her 86 year-old Grandma how to do salsa dancing on the college lawn during the celebrations!

In July of 2006, Hope and John Ayer made a visit to Egremont for Bev's 88th birthday, and a happy family reunion occurred at that time, with various nieces and nephews also there.

It was the Almond's 60th anniversary the following month, so again the family gathered in celebration, with a special meal of Arab food prepared by the family. Grandson Chris Lancaster couldn't make it as by then he was serving in the Marines.

As is often the case in life, celebrations and sad times can be very close to each other; and so it was in November that same year, when Bev's sister Hope was diagnosed with leukemia and died just two weeks later. Hope's family had a service for her in their home town of Cabool, Missouri the day after Thanksgiving. The burial of her ashes was planned for the Kitchen plot in Gilmanton in the summer of 2007, with Harry to conduct the service. Now Beverly had lost both her parents and both her younger sisters as well.

August 2006 – 60th Anniversary
Back: l to r – Rob Lancaster, Chrissy Jones and John Hamlin, Bryan H.
Center: Betsy L., Harry and Beverly, Anne H.
Front: l – Jennifer L.   r – Rebecca H.

CHAPTER 19

The Bletchley Story Re-emerges

*This chapter is inserted here as it spans the period
from the 1970s until the present day.*

In 1974, a book entitled *The Ultra Secret* by F. W.
Winterbotham was published in England and caused quite a
stir. Winterbotham had been a high-ranking member of MI-6
(British Intelligence) and in charge of how Enigma reports coming out of Bletchley Park were used, and thus he knew whereof he
wrote. For the almost 30 years since the war, during which time
it appears the Bletchley Park veterans had not talked publicly to
anyone about what they had done, it came as a shock to many of
them that these top-secret matters were now being shared publicly. There were questions if in fact it was legal or right to share
such information, and lots of uncertainty about sharing themselves what they had pledged never to reveal. One thinks again of
Churchill's remarks about the Bletchley folk being the geese "who
never cackled".

When Beverly's son-in-law, Bryan, heard about the book, he read it and then asked Bev if this was what she had been doing in the war. Not wanting to readily divulge the secrets kept all those years, she simply asked to read the book. After doing so, she did admit to her family that this was in fact what she had worked on at Bletchley.

Soon, more books were written, old Bletchley friends began to find each other, and reunions of various kinds occurred, from the 1980s right up to the 2000s. Beverly has a file filled with correspondence, memoirs, meeting notices, newspaper clippings, and speeches from that time – all to do with getting these veterans together again and sharing their memories of the war. The Association of the Army Special Security Group – 'Old Hands' met, corresponded and shared news and addresses. Old friends wrote letters or visited each other once addresses were collected and shared. And there were several who, like Thomas Parrish, came to visit Bev, or got in touch to interview her for their books on the Bletchley period.

One wonderful reconnection was made in 1992, when Bryan Hamlin met Barbara Eachus, the British Vice-Consul, at an event in Boston. They discovered, to the complete astonishment of both, that Barbara had worked at Bletchley Park during the war, as had her husband, Joe, and that she remembered Beverly from then. Joe Eachus[7] was the American cryptanalyst who had worked with Alan Turing, and Barbara Abernethy, as she was then, had been one of the main administrators at Bletchley – see Chap. 8. She and Joe had met at that time, later married, and eventually settled in the Boston area.

---

7 Joe Eachus went on to become one of the leading computer experts in the post-war US codebreaking organisation, the National Security Agency, where he earned the title of "father of the mainframe". When Eachus left the NSA to join Honeywell in 1955, he remained a member of the NSA scientific advisory board.

So it was a delight for the Hamlins to reunite Bev with these old colleagues later that year, at their Christmas party in Cambridge, MA. They became good friends, and Barbara subsequently kept Bev abreast of much news of former colleagues and of the Bletchley Park property itself. They remained in touch until Barbara's death in 2012. A letter from Bev with memories of their Bletchley days was read by Anne at Barbara's memorial.

Beverly with Joe and Barbara Eachus in Cambridge, MA – Dec. 1992

There were reunions of several of the team from Hut 3 that Bev had been part of, hosted by Bletchley colleague Landis Gores[8] at his home in Connecticut. And in October, 1993, following some correspondence, Telford Taylor and his wife came to lunch with

---

8 Landis Gores had become a noted architect after the war, working with Phillip Johnson, in the modernist style of Wright and Gropius. The home in which these reunions took place was a beautiful example of his work.

Beverly and Harry in North Egremont, a very special reunion indeed. Taylor died in 1998 at age 90.

Beverly was delighted to get back in touch with so many old friends, and began a lively exchange of letters with Mavis Batey (a British friend who has since died), Pauline Burrough Lee (also English), and Annabel Grover Stover (American).

Along with the reconnecting of people and the writing of stories, there was an on-going story unfolding about the actual property of Bletchley Park, which had been moth-balled since the war. The Bletchley Park Trust was set up in the early 1990s to plan how to preserve this extraordinary place; and after many years and much controversy it eventually became a cryptography museum and historic site which is now a popular tourist destination.

In 1992, when Anne and Bryan spent a year in England with their children, they were able to visit Bletchley Park. After this visit, Anne wrote her mother, "Well, well – did we have an amazing day yesterday. You know we'd mentioned trying to have a look at Bletchley Park en route to lunch with friends in Bedford? Well we did just that, though we got there very late, so only had time to look and dash, we thought. When we got there, however, there were soldiers on the gate and we were told we had to get a pass, etc. etc. Bryan finally found and chatted up the main man present, Tony Sale, and it developed that they were having a huge 'open day' gala event that day which we had stumbled upon!! There were exhibits, (including the original Enigma machine on display), military types everywhere, tours, etc. – all, we gathered, to promote the Bletchley Park Trust they have launched to save and restore the place. When we had dropped a few names like Kitchen, Eachus, and T. Taylor – we were instant VIPs, got official guest passes, got a private tour by Mr. Sale of all the buildings you'd have known, etc. It really was totally amazing that we hit upon that day."

Since that time, the legacy of Bletchley Park has been well-preserved, and they have worked hard to collect the stories of those who worked there and to recognize the contributions each made. They have created a Roll of Honor on their website celebrating the veterans of that place.

Then in 2009, the British government decided it was high time that all those who had served in secrecy at Bletchley were properly recognized. Each received a badge from the British Government Code and Cypher School. The accompanying certificate expressed "deepest gratitude for the vital service you performed during World War II", and was signed by the then Prime Minister Gordon Brown. This sits in pride of place in Bev's living room. A photo of the badge is on the back cover of this book.

It is wonderful that Beverly was also recognized in her own country. In May of 2015 she was given an award by the DAR, as part of their American Women in History project, for her service in Britain in WWII. This award came as a complete surprise to her, although it had been carefully planned by her fellow DAR members, via e-mail with Anne, who was the speaker to recount what her mother had done during the war. Beverly delighted in the surprise of it all. The story of the award was carried on the front page of *The Berkshire Record,* a local weekly paper, a few days later. That article resulted in a phone call the next morning, and a meeting with a local man whose father, David Blair, had also worked in Hut 3 at Bletchley and known Beverly there.

One other sign of the resurgence of interest in Bletchley Park is the spate of books that has been produced. *Enigma,* a 1995 novel by Robert Harris, was a popular success and was later made into a movie starring Kate Winslet. Then the afore-mentioned film, *The Imitation Game,* has brought increased awareness of the incredible story of this place. A search for books about Bletchley Park on Amazon recently listed over one thousand books ranging from historical analysis to fiction to memoirs to crossword puzzles. In just the first 60 items of those listings, over 40 of them have been published since 2010, and three more are due to come out in 2016 – showing that interest in Bletchley Park and its part in WWII is strong and growing. And the little lady on Baldwin Hill never ceases to be amazed at how the venture of which she was a part has captivated so many people so many years later.

Beverly with her DAR award, along with Chapter
Regent Margaret Joseph, and Anne

CHAPTER 20

Another Chapter

In 2007, some of the family gathered in Egremont at the end of May for the Memorial Day weekend. Rob, Betsy, and Jenny Lancaster were there from NYC, and Bryan and Anne Hamlin from the Boston suburb of Medford, where they now lived. It was a happy time with good weather, and lots of gardening was done. The New York and Medford contingents went home on Sunday afternoon, and on Monday Harry and Bev took part in the local Memorial Day ceremony where Harry, as he had done many times before, led a prayer. He and Bev later enjoyed tea on their patio, and then went out for dinner and had a lovely time together. Beverly remembers Harry's delightful comment as they drove along, "Here I am, taking my best girlfriend out to dinner!"

On Wednesday morning, May 30, Harry went out as usual to get the newspaper from the box at the roadside, but when he didn't return after a while, Bev went out and found him lying unconscious in the driveway. She had to leave him while going in to phone 911, and on returning outside, there was dear friend and neighbor Peter Goldberg who was out for a walk. Peter went home just long enough to cancel all his appointments for the day and then returned to stay at Bev's side until some of the family could get there. After Bev had phoned the family, Peter took her to the the local hospital where the ambulance had taken Harry. When they sent him on to Berkshire Medical Center in Pittsfield an hour north, Peter drove Beverly there. Meanwhile, Bryan drove to Anne's school to give her the news. Her colleagues there couldn't have been kinder and sent her off at once to be with her parents.

Harry and Bev have fun with the "kissing bears" they were given.

She and Bryan arrived at the hospital early that afternoon and, along with Bev, talked to the doctor and saw the x-rays of Harry's head. Even a non-medic could see that blood had pooled inside his skull, and it was clear this was very serious. The doctor said that surgery could possibly be done, but that even if he survived surgery, there would be long-term brain damage. Beverly immediately asked what parts of his brain were already impacted, and when told it was speech and language areas among others, she was absolutely clear that no surgery would be done, and that Harry should be allowed to die peacefully. They had fully discussed their end-of-life wishes, and she was absolutely certain that that was what he would want. It was a powerful and inspiring thing to see Bev's clarity, which helped all the family at that time. Betsy and Rob arrived later that evening, and Jennifer, Rebecca, and John, with girlfriend Chrissy, were all able to come in the next day or so to say goodbye while Harry was in hospice care in the hospital. He slipped peacefully away without regaining consciousness very early on June 3rd. During those few days the Almonds' Congregational minister, a Jewish friend, and the Muslim chaplain to the hospital all came to pray at his bedside – testament to his decades-long passion for bridge-building between the children of Abraham.

The funeral, a few days later, was also a celebration of his life and faith. As chaplain to the fire department Harry was accorded full honors – including the bringing of his ashes to the church on the fire engine, accompanied by his two grandsons, as Christopher had been able to get leave from the Marines to be present. The firemen also did the ringing of a fire bell at the service, provided a guard of honor at the church, and then gave a lunch at the firehouse for all who could come after the service.

The service that was already planned for Hopie in Gilmanton that summer thus became a double memorial, and when the family gathered for it in July, a dear friend, retired Rev. Alan Macy of Great Barrington, conducted the service for both. It was a precious time of remembering two special lives, for Beverly and for all of those in the next generations, and in the town that held so many happy memories for the family.

It seems fitting to share here two stories about Beverly that typify her attitude to life in the months following Harry's death.

One was shared by her son-in-law Bryan Hamlin. The phone rang at the Hamlin home one day in August or September, and when Bryan answered, it was Beverly saying, "I've just had one of the most wonderful experiences of my life!" He couldn't imagine what she was referring to until she explained how she had just been having tea outside when a black bear walked onto the patio right by her and walked around her chair! Then to Bev's annoyance the bear attacked the hummingbird feeder, no doubt smelling the sugar water, knocking it to the ground. As they continued talking on the phone, Bev exclaimed, "Oh, he's coming back." Bryan confirmed that she was safely inside the house and then urged her to close the glass door to the patio which was still open. What struck Bryan most about the conversation was that her reaction to this event was pure delight and wonder, and no fear at all.

Then in the fall of 2007, Bev's granddaughter Jennifer Lancaster came to stay with her for about four months, thus having a unique insight as to how things were going in that period. She describes that time of a twenty-something and an eighty-nine year old being housemates in this way: "I remember how big-hearted Grandma was, as she always is. She welcomed me into the house with open arms and an open invitation! It shouldn't have been surprising, but somehow it was. Perhaps it was because I was very conscious of my own narrative – how terrified I was of my post-college future, and how poorly I was dealing with an unrequited romance. I think I expected to learn something about heart-break from Grandma and her mourning of Grandpa; I just didn't know what it would be. I remember how faithfully she continued to live her days in the wake of losing her beloved husband, friend, and partner. She adjusted with such grace and elegance of spirit. She was showered with love from friends and family around the world and she took not one bit of it for granted. She was living in a space of deep gratitude. She took almost daily joy in spotting the red cardinal in the trees nearby, certain that Grandpa's spirit was watching out for her.

"I was supposed to be writing my first novel. Every day, Grandma would ask me how it was going. It was close to a reminder some days, but never a scold, sometimes just simply: 'Have you written today?' She never pressed much for details, she never asked to read it. (Possibly I had warned her from the get-go that I would be offering no such drafts for anyone to read.) She listened to my work grievances and stories, we sat lazily with coffee after breakfast at the dining room table, we put little notes on the kitchen counter when one or the other of us left the house, we cooked funny and strange small meals for ourselves, we sat wrapped in blankets and doing crossword puzzles on into the late evening. As I remember it, she left me a note and a plate of cookies beside it every night I had a later shift at work. Quintessential Grandma."

What a delightful picture Jennifer paints of this unexpected pair sharing their lives so lovingly and happily at a time of transition for both of them.

CHAPTER 21

Beverly today

At the time of Harry's death, both he and Beverly were 88 years old, and they had been married for almost 61 years of adventures. Now she was on her own, and once again creating a new landscape in which to live her life. Although her loss and grief were deep and real, Beverly's faith was her rock – helping her feel gratitude at how quickly and peacefully Harry had gone, able to appreciate the precious days they had together just before his fall, and most of all believing he was in a better place and re-united with his parents and younger brother, as well as many other loved ones. She does feel that cardinals are somehow their special birds, and each time she sees one she senses his presence in a joyful way.

At some point in her 80s, Beverly had said to her family, "There are three things that are really important to me and keep me going – my 3 F's: Faith, Family, and Friends." That was a wonderful and true statement, and those things continue to be central to all she does. But in her early 90s she amended this to say, "I want to make it 5 Fs, because I'm adding Fun and Food!" That sums up her attitude to life at this point – deep-seated faith, care and contact with family and friends, and a healthy enjoyment of good food and good times as well. She turned 97 in 2015, and her activities are still legion.

Egremont Christmas 2011
left to right – Chris, Rob, Betsy. John and Chrissy standing. Bev, Anne, Bryan. Front – Jenny, Rebecca, Tom (with puppy Charlie)

Commitment to her church is very important to Beverly. She attends every service and event; serves on the Mission Committee; proofreads the church newsletter each month for Pastor Charles Van Ausdall; helps to prepare for and serve meals on special occasions; visits and calls shut-ins and the sick (and recently was made an honorary deacon for doing that so faithfully); regularly attends Bible study groups and a book club; and contributes weekly to the local food bank.

Each day begins with a time of meditation and reflection – giving time for any thoughts that may come. And every night she prays for all the long list of those she cares about. That no doubt helps Bev to have a special link to the Almighty, so when a thought about someone does come into her mind, she acts on it. Once when Bryan and Anne were visiting – she told them at breakfast that she was surprised she hadn't heard from a friend at church – so she called her right away, only to discover that the lady had been taken to the hospital the day before and was in the ICU. Bev immediately informed the pastor and another friend in the church prayer group, and went to visit that afternoon.

Bev is active in the local DAR chapter (and was the Chaplain for some time) and goes to their monthly meetings; and she has continued to meet with a group that were a League of Women Voters chapter, which disbanded as such but still call themselves 'the remnants' and have regular lunches. She has recently joined another monthly women's group called the Thursday Morning Club that meet to hear speakers and have tea together, as well as raising money for scholarships and other community needs.

In early 2015, Beverly joined a balance class in her town with other seniors and enjoyed interacting and sharing with them, and did the assigned exercises faithfully. Whenever the weather permits, she goes for a walk up the hill on which she lives, turning around and walking backwards for a while when the incline gets steep – which gives delight to her neighbors and causes consternation to passers-by.

Bev is deeply engaged in local politics and attends Town Meetings and many Select Board meetings to keep abreast of events. Along with good friends Tom and Juliet Haas and others they plan on who they think should be the candidates for any open town position and then campaign actively. Once, Beverly saw a campaign sign on the lawn of a friend and was shocked, because she knew both that her friend was away, and that she wouldn't support that candidate, so she just pulled up the sign and stuck it in the trunk of her car! Someone who saw this happen called the police to complain, but Bev explained and was forgiven for the deed.

She is an excellent baker, and her bread, apple pies, and cookies of various kinds are popular not only with the family and neighbors – but at local bake sales and church events. Her deviled eggs are regular items at neighborhood gatherings and always vanish fast. And she frequently invites friends and neighbors over for a meal or tea.

Beverly keeps up with world events to an astonishing degree – pouring over the *Berkshire Eagle* daily (although she is frustrated with its recent changes and paring down!), watching PBS News Hour every night, as well as other news shows on PBS at other times. She clips out articles she thinks might be of interest to family and friends and mails them off. And she has no hesitation in writing to editors, news people, and others when she has a strong reaction to something seen or read. She almost always has questions on matters of national or global concern that she wants to discuss when family members visit.

Crossword puzzles are a special interest and Bev does them daily. She watches *Jeopardy* on TV most nights and tries to get the answers. She knits afghan squares and pieces them together to make blankets for family members and for nursing homes. And she is an avid reader – usually having multiple books on the go at once, including some to read daily in her morning quiet time as devotionals; whatever book her book club is reading; another novel as a back-up if she needs a change; and often a biography or current events book to keep her informed. She has also read several books in French in recent years, mostly memoirs of Swiss or French friends, and does so with the dictionary at her side to help her through.

Beverly at home, reading in her favorite chair
(photo credit – Caroline Donsbough)

Not only is Bev's appreciation for reading and words strong, but her use of language regularly delights those who talk with her. Words or phrases such as 'pantywaist' (Chap. 3), or 'laid him out in lavender' (Chap. 8), are unexpected to a younger generation, as was the expression 'hidden wisdom' Beverly used to describe wearing long underwear one very cold day. One never knows quite what new and delightful expressions will emerge.

But most of all her life continues to be about people – those she sees and visits locally, family – wherever they are, and friends around the country and around the world that she writes to regularly and phones on occasion. All of the above are included in her daily prayers. She is often teased that she single-handedly keeps the US Postal Service in operation due to the volume of her writing. Bev keeps a basket of mail she's received that she thinks might be of interest to the family to read when they visit. Much of the mail she receives includes references to cards or notes she has sent and expressing how much they meant. She hears regularly from friends in Switzerland, Britain, Canada, Australia, and India, for example.

As mentioned above, her family is one of Beverly's basic 'Five Fs', and she is very proud of the work and accomplishments of each person in it. She follows with great interest Betsy's new career as Senior Executive Associate at the Asia Society, beginning in 1999; and also Anne's new role when she returned to her first love as a teacher in 2001. Granddaughter Rebecca Hamlin teaches political science at the University of Massachusetts in Amherst, is married to Tom Annese, and in 2013 they had a daughter, Althea Beverly, Bev's first great-grandchild. Chris Lancaster, having left the US Marine Corps after nine years, continues his work in aviation electronics, lives in Arizona, and married Irma Garcia in 2015, bringing two more great grandchildren into the family, William and Michael (aged 6 and 2). John Hamlin works with the Bank of New York Mellon in financial services, and lives with his wife Chrissy in Maine; and Jennifer, having graduated with a master's degree in social work, is working with foster children in New York City. Bev also keeps in touch with her many nieces and nephews and their families.

On Bev's 97th birthday, with daughter Anne, granddaughter
Rebecca, and great-granddaughter Althea

Her files include those labeled "Things to keep – Important"
and "Things to keep – Sentimental", and the latter is stuffed with
precious letters from loved ones.

Not only is a basket of letters kept out by Bev for visiting family to read, but there is also a "To Do" list on the kitchen counter
with jobs for them to deal with. She is not shy about asking for
help as needed, either from family or from her neighbors!

Beverly keeps in touch with Middle East friends as well. Amal
was a college friend of Anne's from Jordan in the 1960s, and she

and Bev still talk on the phone and write at regular intervals. Fareed from Iraq met Harry and Beverly when he was working at Harvard, and he now serves as an Ambassador in the Iraqi diplomatic corps. Bev frequently asks the Hamlins to e-mail him her greetings, and ask after him, and let him know she prays for him and his work. He always responds with appreciation and feels it makes a difference. And those are but two examples.

Any opportunity is also taken to connect with and share wisdom with those she meets randomly. Not long ago Bev was waiting in a gas station and saw that a young man next to her was smoking. She turned to him and said something like, "You know, I used to smoke, but I stopped when I was about your age, and I'm very glad I did." The fellow was quite intrigued and asked how old she was now. When she said 96 – he was stunned and promptly asked if he could give her a hug! Of course she said yes! Who knows if it gave him pause on the smoking – but one can be pretty sure he'll remember the encounter.

Not surprisingly, her care for others is also wonderfully given back to her. There are many friends who will pick her up and take her to events in bad weather or after dark when she doesn't drive. These include Egremont neighbors and also many friends from her church, such as Connie Friedrich, Grace Zabell, and the Veits. Neighbors on Baldwin Hill will drop by for tea or a visit and often bring her soup, meals, or produce from their gardens. Chuck Ogden, a local friend who calls her his 'second mother' often drops by to visit and help Bev with various tasks in the house. Some of the other caring neighbors who have helped her in many ways include the Herbers, Haases, Elliotts, Blancos, Proctors, Pat Murtaugh, and the Goldbergs. The whole town threw her a huge surprise 96th birthday party in the park (organized by Robin Goldberg and others) to which about 60 people turned up – complete with live music, a potluck supper, a huge cake, flower arrangements for each table made by the garden club, and culminating with the fire department arriving on their trucks to give her hugs and share their memories of Harry.

It seems fitting to close this story of an ageless adventurer with some Bible verses from the book of Proverbs that summarize the life of this amazing woman.

A wife of noble character who can find? She is worth far more than rubies.

Her husband has full confidence in her and lacks nothing of value.

She is clothed with strength and dignity; she can laugh at the days to come.

She speaks with wisdom, and faithful instruction is on her tongue.

She watches over the affairs of her household and does not eat the bread of idleness.

Her children arise and call her blessed; her husband also, and he praises her:

"Many women do noble things, but you surpass them all."

Charm is deceptive, and beauty is fleeting; but a woman who fears the Lord is to be praised.

Honor her for all that her hands have done, and let her works bring her praise at the city gate.

It is perfect that laughter is included in these traits of a good woman, because Bev's zest for life and sense of humor continue strong, as do her faith, her curiosity, and her care.

Beverly, age 97, in 2015 (photo credit – Caroline Donsbough)

APPENDIX

A Brief History of the Oxford Group and MRA

When writing about a movement or organization that has endured close to one hundred years in various forms and with changing names, leaders and programs – it is hard to be both brief and accurate. As background and context to the work that Beverly Kitchen Almond and her family were part of, the following may help.

Frank N.D. Buchman, a Lutheran minister born in Pennsylvania in 1878, spent his early adult years doing evangelical youth ministry in the United States as well as in India, China and Britain. He travelled widely and worked with the YMCA, and with many well-known preachers of his day, and also met people of many nationalities and backgrounds. By the 1930s, because of his work with students, including many at Oxford University in England, his work became known as the Oxford Group. Buchman and his colleagues challenged people to face themselves honestly, change their lives with God's help, and then work to help others do the same. They also encouraged those they met to take time in quiet reflection daily to find guidance for their lives. This work grew to the extent that it was drawing crowds of thousands to meetings and house-parties across Europe and the United States by the 1930s. In this period, it also helped give birth to the Alchoholics Anonymous (AA) movement, in which Bev's father had a founding role.

In 1938, as the world uneasily faced the perils leading to WWII and nations built up stockpiles of arms, Buchman felt the need to express a concept that went beyond the personal, and he called for "moral and spiritual re-armament", a force powerful enough to re-make the world. Thus he launched the idea of Moral Re-Armament (MRA), which is what the movement became known as from then on. French philosopher Gabriel Marcel described Buchman's vision as going from "the intimate to the global".

From the simple beginning of a mission to turn around the lives of individual students, this idea and the team that carried it forward grew greatly. From the 1940s into the 1960s there were large conference centers set up in the USA, Switzerland, England and India, as well as many smaller centers around the world, such as at Dellwood, the Almonds' home for eleven years. The immediate post-war years saw effective work in helping bring Germany and Japan back into the family of nations. MRA became active in about thirty countries on all continents. Plays and musicals were used to get across the ideas, and groups traveled to present them in many countries. There was an interesting combination of focus on the importance of individuals changing, along with strategic planning to reach leaders of various kinds, including in government, labor, industry, and the arts.

Following several years of increasing incapacity, Buchman died in 1961. He was succeeded by British writer Peter Howard who himself died quite suddenly just four years later, plunging the work into crisis.

In the United States, in part because of the anti-communist sentiments of many during and following the McCarthy period, MRA had become more conservative. There was also fear of young people going astray in the era of sexual freedom, drugs and the whole counter-culture movement. Following a large youth conference at the MRA conference center on Mackinac Island in 1964, a show was created, "Sing-Out", which challenged and inspired many young people with a positive alternative for change, and which then began touring. By the summer of 1965 this had become a huge endeavor with "Sing-Outs" springing up in many places. It became a movement in and of itself and spread to some other countries as well through the MRA network. Eventually the Sing-Outs evolved into "Up With People" (UWP), incorporated as such in 1968. Other programs of MRA in the USA were ended in order to give full support to UWP. The conference center on Mackinac Island was turned into a college which lasted only four years, and then the property was sold. Dellwood and other properties around the country were also sold. Many older people who had worked with MRA were told they were not needed by UWP, and quite suddenly had to go and find new careers.

These developments were met with growing concern amongst other MRA groups, particularly in Britain. Extra effort was put into maintaining the summer conferences at Caux, Switzerland; and starting in 1967, a new conference center was developed at Panchgani, India through the leadership of Rajmohan Gandhi, a grandson of the Mahatma.

In 1971 a small group from Britain visited Canada and the US to explore interest in reviving MRA in North America. This led to a modest New Year conference in Trois Rivieres, Quebec in January 1972, which the Almond family attended, fresh from their return from Lebanon. Harry Almond worked with some older MRA folk, and with two young Americans who had met MRA while Rhodes scholars at Oxford, Dick Ruffin and Steve Dickinson; and by 1976, MRA USA was reborn. After many years headquartered in Washington DC, in 2007 the head office moved to Richmond, Virginia where effective work has been done now for some decades under the banner "Hope in the Cities". In 1999 the world work of MRA changed its name to Initiatives of Change (IofC). It continues to be active in many countries with a variety of programs.

For Further Reading

Victor Kitchen and AA

Kitchen, V. C., *I Was A Pagan*, New York, Harper and Brothers, 1934.

B., Dick, *The Oxford Group and Alcoholics Anonymous*, Kihei HI, Paradise Research Publications, 1998.

Chesnut, Glenn F., *Changed By Grace: Vic Kitchen, The Oxford Group and AA*, Lincoln NE, iUniverse, 2006.

Related to Glenn Chesnut's book: http://hindsfoot.org/kchange3.html

Harry Almond

Almond, Harry J., *An American in the Middle East*, Caux Books, 2009.

Contact: HJAbooks@gmail.com for information on how to acquire any of Harry Almond's books.

Bletchley Park

Hinsley, F.H. and Stripp, Alan (editors), *Codebreakers: The Inside Story of Bletchley Park*, New York, Oxford University Press, 1993.

McKay, Sinclair, *The Secret Lives of Codebreakers*, New York, Penguin, 2010.

Parrish, Thomas, *The Ultra Americans*, Briarcliff Manor NY, Stein and Day, 1986.

http://www.bletchleypark.org.uk

MRA/Initiatives of Change

Lean, Garth, *On the Tail of a Comet: The Life of Frank Buchman*, Colorado Springs, Helmers and Howard, 1988
(originally published in London, England by Constable Publishers as: *Frank Buchman: A Life,*1985)

Johnston, Douglas and Samson, Cynthia (editors), *Religion: The Missing Dimension of Statecraft* (particularly chapters 4 and 10*)*, New York, Oxford University Press, 1994.

website: usiofc.org
https://en.wikipedia.org/wiki/Moral_Re-Armament

Author Biography

Beverly Anne Hamlin chronicles Beverly Almond's adventures from the unique perspective of both daughter and friend.

Born in Iraq, Anne earned her BA from Beirut College for Women while her family was living in Lebanon. She worked in international conflict resolution and peacemaking for many years and traveled widely during that time. Hamlin later earned an MA in education from Lesley University in Cambridge, Massachusetts, before starting a second career as an elementary school teacher.

Now retired, Anne enjoys having more time for photography and family. She and her husband Bryan Hamlin live near Boston, in Medford, MA, and are the proud grandparents of Beverly Almond's first great-grandchild.

Made in the USA
Charleston, SC
09 March 2016